0 XI/00
8 X 1/05 LT 10/04
13 X 6/10 LT 3/10

California
School Rules

School Wise Press is dedicated to helping parents get smart about California schools (K–12). Toward that end, we publish county guidebooks to public schools, school profiles, and custom school-selection reports, all designed to help parents choose schools with facts in their hands. In addition, we publish reference books and "how-to" guides like this one, which we hope will encourage and enable parents to play the school game wisely. Our Web site—www.schoolwisepress.com— offers a wealth of information and ideas about schools, including a virtual library, news articles, a legislative alert, and comparative rankings of schools in every county in California. In addition, the Web site includes a regular school law column by Judy Goddess, the author of this book. She welcomes you to visit her there weekly.

OTHER WORDS OF PRAISE
FOR *CALIFORNIA SCHOOL RULES*

"For students, the 'customers' of the education system, *California School Rules* is the perfect tool for self-advocacy. This book can provide any student with a background that will allow him to address his concerns about school in a responsible and mature way. *California School Rules* should be required reading for every student!"

— Nickolas Rodriguez, State Officer
of the California Association of Student Councils

"*California School Rules* is filled with useful information, the kind which well-intentioned administrators often presume to be too complex or technical for most parents. This book will fill the information gap. Better informed parents will help us all down the road to better schools, not just for their own kids, but for all kids."

— Jill Wynns, Member of
San Francisco Unified School District Board of Education,
and Director of the California School Boards Association

California School Rules

A SCHOOL-SMART PARENT'S GUIDE TO ADVOCATING FOR YOUR CHILD

JUDY GODDESS, PH.D

SCHOOL WISE PRESS

School Wise Press
236 Moncada Street
San Francisco, CA 94127
(4150) 337-7971
e-mail: info@schoolwisepress.com

School Wise Press is an imprint of Publishing 20/20

Editor: Steve Rees
Production Managment: BookMatters
Compositor and text designer: BookMatters
Cover designer: Linda M. Wanczyk
Copyeditor: Pictures & Words
Proofreader: Rebecca Davenport
Indexer: Janet Vail
Printing: Data Reproductions

Library of Congress Cataloging-in-Publication Data
Goddess, Judy.
    California School Rules : a school-smart parent's guide to advocating for your child / Judy Goddess.
        p.   cm.
    Includes bibliographical references and index.
    ISBN 1-887836-10-1
        1. Educational law and legislation—California—Popular works.
2. Students—Legal status, laws, etc.—California—Popular works.
3. Parent-teacher relationships—Law and legislation—California—
Popular works. 4. Education, Elementary—Parent participation—
California.   I. Title.
KFC648.Z9G63   1997
344.794'07—dc21   97-26487
                                                                        CIP

10 9 8 7 6 5 4 3 2 1

Contents

to mainstream children • more attention paid to special ed needs • neglect of mainstream students • support in IEP meeting

Part II: The Players
Teachers, Parents, Students, and Principals

Part III: Expanding Rights, Expanding Choices

Appendices

Introduction

At one time, schoolhouse doors were barred to parents. Parents could not visit classes or question a principal's disciplinary decisions. Curriculum decisions were considered to be beyond our grasp. Nor could parents challenge a specialist's assignment of their child to a remedial class. Authority was held entirely by each school's principal and teaching staff. Parents hoped for a principal who was fair and had an open mind. But if he was neither fair nor open-minded, they had no recourse.

Fortunately, much has changed since then. After many years of parent organizing and voting for reform-minded school board candidates, and decades of research documenting the many benefits of greater parent involvement in their children's education, not the least of which is that children of involved parents tend to be more academically successful, parents are being "welcomed" as participants in school life in entirely new ways. Participation now includes a seat at the table when the school is developing its annual plan and the budget to realize it; when the school is developing its discipline code; and when new programs are designed and evaluated. These are decisions of some consequence. And they are decisions that now legally require parent involvement.

There is also a pragmatic dimension to this new era of greater parent participation in running schools. Proposition 13 has meant twenty years of limited resources for California schools. Educators' newly extended welcome to parents from within the castle of education is, to some degree, born of this necessity. Sensing that we are more welcome now, parents are taking bolder steps into the world our children inhabit. This is, to be sure, a good thing.

This more hopeful period is also marked by a fair number of new laws that redefine the legal terrain in ways that favor parents more fully. Just sample a few of these reforms. Parents now have, among other rights, the right to choose which school their child will attend, the right to request that their limited-English speaking child be taught in a bilingual program, the right to reject district assignment of their child to special education programs, and the right to defend their child at a pre-suspension conference.

While these are changes for the better, they are reversible on short notice, as evidenced by the most recent election results—which drastically limited parent involvement in placement decisions around bilingual education. The California legislature deserves more attention than we give it. With education issues remaining a hot political potato, and with parents lacking a lobby of our own, we are unusually vulnerable to rude surprises.

A few words about my own experience are in order. Many years ago in Chicago, I defended the rights of children who wanted desperately to learn, but instead were largely untaught or, even worse, spurned by a school district that should have served them. I remember the mother of a 15-year-old young man who had been repeatedly tested for special education but never placed; the 6-year-old who was sexually abused by her teacher; the 15-year-old whom the high school wanted to send back to elementary school because he was so "immature"; and the parents of an 11-year-old who struggled valiantly to defend the competence of their child against a room full of educational "experts" who had consigned him to a program for mentally retarded youngsters.

Then I moved to California, where I worked on other issues. Yet, I continued to be most moved by the daily repetition of injustices meted out to unwitting students and their parents. In my advocacy work here in California, I encountered anxious single mothers repeatedly reminded by teachers (ironically often single parents themselves) of the "inevitability" of their children's problems; immigrants with limited language skills who were never informed of the options available for their children; brilliant Latino youths labeled as gang members by district officials and treated accordingly; and school officials who turned deaf ears to the repeated pleas of low-income parents.

This book is a natural by-product of this work. As an advocate, but also as a mother, I understand how frustrated, how disappointed, how enraged a parent can become when trying to advocate her child's cause. One of my greatest frustrations came from not knowing the rules of the game, trapped in a bureaucracy that relies on rules—and parents' ignorance of them—as excuses for not helping our children. It's this single frustration that I hope this book will remedy. My entire purpose is to enable you to play the school game smart. Quite simply, this book lets parents know their school rights, the conflicts that are likely to arise, who has the legal authority to decide their outcome, what you can do to influence the result, and, if need be, how to appeal these decisions.

Welcome to a seat at the table. I hope you find this book to be a useful guide to the rules of the school game.

The Basics

What Is Taught

1 Curriculum and Instruction

"Angry parents storm school board meeting," headlines yet another front-page article on what students don't know. Can't read . . . can't write . . . can't spell . . . don't know their times tables . . . can't do word problems . . . and on and on.

The discontents of professional educators usually don't rate a front page, yet they, too, present a list of "don't know's." Students don't know their history . . . geography . . . Shakespeare . . . can't follow a science text . . . speak a foreign language . . . qualify for freshman math and English classes in college . . . or hold their own with young people from other nations. Sometimes the official responses are equally dramatic: distinguished members of state advisory committees are dumped . . . textbook selection processes are questioned . . . standardized tests are rejected.

What, in fact, should students be learning? Are they learning it? If not, why not? How does your child's school compare with other schools in the city, the state, across the country and around the world? And what about special programs—programs for the gifted, for students whose skills are not up to grade level, vocational training?

All levels of government—federal, state, and your local school board—have a voice in curriculum decisions. National commissions announce educational standards and champion educational goals. State-level task forces draft standards for subject matter areas. English and math standards were adopted in 1997; the California Board of Education will consider draft standards for history and science in 1998. Curriculum frameworks, developed from these standards, suggest classroom lessons and activities, and detail the knowledge and skills expected of students in all grade levels. The approved standards will be the basis of the Spring 1999 statewide standardized exam currently under development. (See chapter 2, "Assessment.") Additionally, the standards and frameworks inform the textbook selection process. All of these activities—standards, frameworks, and the standardized exam—are aimed at improving student achievement, and at holding schools and teachers accountable for student progress.

Although national directives and decisions at the state level certainly shape the curriculum, most curriculum decisions are made at the district level. Under California school law, districts are given the freedom to evaluate instructional materials and to adopt resources that meet the needs of their students, as long as these choices comply with the education code. It is this emphasis on local control that enables you as a parent to raise questions about what is taught. At times, you may air your individual questions and concerns to a teacher or principal at one school and find satisfaction. At others, you may raise questions before a larger public, the school site council perhaps, or the PTA or the school board. The point is, you have more than one place to turn to for a hearing of your concerns.

Despite the advantages of local control of curriculum, it does present two inherent disadvantages. First, there may be no coherent vision of what students are expected to know and be able to do. Second, local districts have limited accountability to higher-level authorities. If you don't find satisfaction at the local level, you'll be hard-pressed to find anyone who can act on your concerns at the county or state level.

This chapter addresses parent questions of two types. The first is the sort that keeps parents awake at night. Is my child "getting it"? Is she reading at grade level? Is my son keeping up with the rest of the math class? Is my child really understanding American history? These are questions about your child's successful mastery of a curriculum that you accept.

The second category of parent questions delves into the realm of curriculum with which you do not agree. You may not agree with what is being taught, or how a subject is being taught. You may wonder why something that you believe *should* be taught has been omitted from the curriculum. Or you may question why courses offered to some students are not being offered to your child. These questions, while different, summon up an intensity of feeling and belief in all parents who share similar concerns. If you are among them, it helps to keep in mind the great range of choices you have in your search for answers. Teachers differ. Schools differ. Principals differ. Curriculum development specialists differ. Even school board members are likely to differ in their attitudes toward policy. Those differences often give you an opportunity to find your way around curriculum policies with which you do not agree.

As you read through the following questions and answers, you'll gain a greater understanding of how those differences might benefit you and your child. Even better, you'll come to know more about who has the authority to make the changes you're pursuing.

Questions and Answers

Math basics

1. *My daughter is in the fourth grade and she still doesn't know her multiplication tables. Most of her other classmates don't either. Who decided that 10-year-olds don't need to learn their times tables?*

The math framework, published by the state, is very clear: fourth-graders should know their times tables and be able to demonstrate proficiency in a number of computational skills. Your school or district should have a copy of the Department of Education's Math Framework, or you could order a copy from Sacramento. (Request the 1998 edition, which reflects the board's 1997 decision on math standards and instructional methods.) After you have reviewed the framework and talked with other parents, ask the principal to schedule a parents' meeting to review the curriculum. Because math has been such a contentious issue, some schools schedule parent "math nights"[1] at which teachers explain the curriculum and conduct demonstration lessons. These sessions help anxious parents support their child's learning, by modeling appropriate questions and providing strategies for parents to help with their child's homework.

Ban the Counters!

Sonoma Valley school officials recently banned calculators in kindergarten through third-grade classrooms. Fourth and fifth-graders may use calculators for special "enhancement" projects, but first the students must demonstrate that they know their tables. The school board admits that Sonoma may be the only district in the state with such a ban.

You're clearly not the only parent who's hopped up about math. Even school board meetings on the math curriculum can turn into shouting matches.

"Theory is fine, but what about the times tables?" demanded the Palo Alto middle school parents who support basic computational skills.

"Rote memorization is the surest way to kill any interest in the beauty of math," retorted the supporters of more concept-based math. "Math should develop the child's ability to problem-solve, to use reason and logic."

Disputes like this one in Palo Alto can be heard in districts throughout the state and the country, as parents express anger that the curriculum innovations that promise so much seem to leave their children behind.[2] (Incidentally, the math standards adopted in late 1997 emphasize basic computational skills.)

<u>Reading skills</u>

   2. *My son can't read. He's ready for middle school, but when I take*
      him to the store he can't read even simple labels. What can I do?

While parents can contribute to their children's learning, the schools are responsible for teaching them. Parents cannot be expected to provide the school curriculum at home.

There are many reasons why children have problems learning to read. Ask your son what he thinks the problem might be. He may find it difficult to concentrate on his lessons, or perhaps he learns best with a different teaching method. The teaching strategies may be inconsistent from grade to grade—one year whole language, the next phonics, and so on. There may be too many students in the class to allow for the individualized instruction your child might need to succeed.

In 1995, fourth-graders from California tied with fourth-graders from Louisiana for the lowest reading scores in the nation. This poor showing inspired an immediate and strong response from Sacramento. In 1996, Governor Wilson earmarked an additional $770 million to reduce class sizes to 20 or fewer students in the lower grades (K–3) where reading is taught. At the same time, legislation was passed setting aside more than $150 million in additional aid for textbooks and professional-development programs that stress phonics-based teaching methods—sounding out words, spelling, and the mechanics of reading—as opposed to a more literature-based approach, called "whole language." That money was also targeted at K–3 classrooms and teachers.

Schools often suggest placement in a special education class as the answer for children with reading problems. Do not allow this to happen until: (a) other less permanent strategies have been tried; (b) your child has been tested and found to need a special education program; and (c) you and the school have agreed on the type of extra support your child will receive in that program. What you don't want to happen is for your child to be placed in a slower track with lowered expectations. While special education can be very helpful for some children, it is an inappropriate response to inadequate teaching. (See chapter 4, "Special Education.")

> **Time Out for Reading**
>
> Miller Creek Middle School in Marin County closes down every day after lunch for 15 minutes to allow everyone to read—students, teachers, bus drivers, the custodian, secretary, principal, other administrators. There's an emergency phone line, in case you really have to reach someone during that time. "We think reading's important, and it's one way to demonstrate it."

As for what you can do at home, continue to involve your son in reading activities—labels, comics, word games, game instructions, computers, the sports section, lists, letters, messages, books—anything, just as long as he reads. You may also want to find a private tutor. After-school tutoring programs are often organized by community agencies, churches, and universities. You may also want to have your child evaluated by an outside specialist to help you and the school identify the nature of your child's problems and some strategies for addressing them. The Parent Educational Resource Center can provide referrals throughout the state.[3]

Limited access to books

3. My child isn't allowed to take her books home to study. How do schools expect students to learn?

First, I would determine whether this "no books go home" policy is applied to all students in the school, or all schools in the district, or only to certain students or particular schools. Some schools allow students from better neighborhoods to take books home, while denying that right to students from poorer areas. This is neither fair nor legal.

If the policy is applied across the board, I'm afraid I can't give you a very reassuring answer. Schools are reluctant to let students take books home because they are afraid they might get lost and there is no money to replace them. The lack of materials is very near the top of any teacher's list of complaints. (Note that even though there are not enough books, schools may not charge students a "borrowing" fee.) To encourage students to study at home when books are in short supply, some schools allow students to borrow out-of-date readers; others limit homework to worksheets, frequently prepared and copied after hours by teachers, sometimes even at their own expense.

Private organizations are stepping in to address the problem. The California Community Foundation recently announced a new million-dollar initiative to tackle the textbook shortage in the Los Angeles schools. Virgil Roberts, the foundation's vice chairman, said, "At some schools it was a pretty acute situation where they're short by 35 percent to 50 percent of the books they need. When you're short that number of books, forget about homework." [4]

On a much smaller scale, the Children's Book Project in San Francisco annually organizes book drives and distributes more than 20,000 used children's books to classrooms and other children's centers so that students may take books home, whether for the extra study opportunity or for the pure pleasure of reading.[5] It shouldn't be necessary to organize a bake sale to raise money for something as fundamental as books.

Money for Books

California school districts receive $29.05 for books per year for every student in grades K–8, and $19.01 per student for students in grades 9–12. While this is more generous than many other states, it is nowhere near enough. Many of our classrooms have no dictionaries. In others, students use books whose authors are still waiting for people to land on the moon, or refer to countries like the Belgian Congo that no longer exist. Libraries are also in bad shape. The California School Library Association estimates that only about 30 percent of California school libraries have professional librarians, compared to 79 percent of the schools in the rest of the nation.

Project-based instruction

4. *I really like my child's middle school—the teachers, the principal, even the building. I have just one complaint: all they do in their social studies class is projects. For example, instead of studying ancient civilizations, the class spent two months constructing an architectural model of the Parthenon, and another two months building a pyramid. My daughter is an expert now with paste and scissors, but she knows nothing about these civilizations. What do I do?*

Discuss your concerns with your daughter's social studies teacher. Curriculum experts encourage middle school teachers to involve their students in active learning—what's called "hands-on education"—rather than relying solely on textbooks and worksheets. Projects are a prime example of these activities. They can provide academic content while still giving students time to interact with their friends, a key concern of this age group. Projects are also very useful in terms of classroom management, allowing students of varying skill levels to work together and giving teachers time to interact individually with students. In addition, they are less affected by student absences.

But while projects may hold students' attention initially, education is more than fun and games. If the teacher does not connect the activity to the curriculum—constructing a model of the Parthenon, for example, can be related to lessons about forms of government—projects can be a real waste of time.

You and your daughter's teacher should each gain some insight through this exchange. You may also want to join the school district's curriculum review committee.

No time for teaching

5. *The curriculum's fine, but I don't think there's enough time for teaching. The class is just getting started when it's time to move on to the next subject. Anything parents can do?*

Scheduling a day full of 45-minute class periods is not the only option. Many schools, particularly middle and high schools, use block scheduling, in which classes meet for longer periods—90 minutes, for example—and not all classes meet every day. This can be especially helpful when classes require set-up time, as is the case with science labs. But scheduling longer classes is a practical way to increase what teachers call "time on task," those precious moments of focused attention on the subject at hand. With longer classes, less time is lost shuffling between classes, and getting settled at the beginning of class.

There is another issue here that deserves attention: the number of hours in the school year. For several years now, the Sacramento parents' group, Community Partners for Educational Excellence (CPEE), has been waging a campaign to convince their district and the state to increase the minimum school year from its current level of 180 four-hour days.[6] They argue that this abbreviated school year, which provides just 700 hours of instruction, contributes to the comparatively poor achievement scores earned by California students, particularly after one subtracts the days lost to teacher professional development, preparing report cards, parent conferences, holidays, field trips, exams, year-end parties, and early graduation.

Higher graduation requirements

6. *Our district wants to increase the requirements for high school graduation to add more science, math, and foreign language courses. Can they do that?*

Yes, they can. Every school board has the authority to increase the minimum graduation requirements established by the state. Most often, districts have increased requirements so that their students may qualify for the U.C. system. The Challenge initiative, a fairly new state program to improve academic standards and school accountability, requires participating districts to adopt more rigorous graduation requirements. As of November 1997, fifty-seven districts had signed on to become challenge districts, and another 100 districts had expressed interest in the program. Graduation requirements in challenge districts include: four years of English, three years of history, two years of math, two years of lab sciences, one year of foreign language, one year of visual or performing arts, and one course each in health education, career preparation, and service learning.[7]

Desirable as it may be to prepare California's high school students to enter the state's top colleges, stiffer graduation requirements may prevent some students from graduating at all, particularly if these increased requirements are not accompanied by additional academic support. In light of these concerns, the legislature appealed to local school boards to carefully consider the needs of all students before making such a significant change, and to involve parents "broadly reflective of the socioeconomic composition of the district" in this decision.[8]

> **Minimum California requirements for high school graduation—1997–1998 school year.**
>
> • three years of English
> • two years of math
> • one year each of biology and physical sciences
> • three years of social studies
> • one year of art or performing arts, or a foreign language
> • two years of physical education
> • plus passing a district-designed proficiency exam

While it would be wonderful if all California students could meet the entry requirements for the State's best four-year colleges, even those schools that offer the appropriate courses may limit these courses to "certain students." A study of high school graduates conducted several years ago by the Achievement Council indicated that almost 85 percent of African-American and Latino students had not taken the coursework required to enter a four-year college.[9]

Bring back the arts

7. *Who decided that middle school students don't have to study music? I think the arts are important and my child really enjoys them. What can I do?*

The issue is money. While music and art courses are required in elementary schools—where they are often taught by the classroom teacher—they are optional courses for students in grades 7–12. Many people share your concern, including the state board. In its recently released 1997 report on arts education, the board recommended that high-quality, comprehensive arts programs be required in every school. Courses in the arts, they concluded, are valuable both for their ability to awaken students' imagination and creativity, and as the hook that keeps some students in school.

If your concern is shared by other parents from the school, you need to ask the principal and the school site council to consider how these programs might be provided. You might consider hiring a practicing artist who could offer this training, at least for some limited period of time. While all classes offered during the school day must be supervised by a credentialed teacher, or a teacher on waiver (see chapter 5, "Educators and Their 'Customers'"), the principal could assign a credentialed teacher to supervise the class, or it could be available as part of an after-school program. Many schools have turned to the California Arts Council and its Artists in the School Program for financial support.[10]

Computer resources

8. *My son's high school needs more computers. The school only has one computer for every 28 students, a far cry from the district's average of one for every 10. My son is only able to use a computer for research in the library, and even then he usually has to wait in line. What can parents do to get more computers for the school?*

The effort to bring computer hardware into your high school is going to be easy compared to the difficulty of the full effort to bring technology knowledge to the school's students. To accomplish the grander task, you'll need a curriculum, delivered by teachers who themselves have been well educated in the appropriate use of technology, who in turn are supported by information systems specialists who know how to put all this stuff together and keep it running. Of course, you'll also need software, networking equipment, and telecommunications equipment and phone lines if your son and his fellow students are to have access to the internet. All this takes money, time, and a major commitment by parents, students, and the staff leadership of the high school.

You might begin by challenging the unfair distribution of technology resources within your school district. The district has close to an average amount of computer systems per student, so they're doing okay. But they have not fairly shared those resources with your high school.

I recommend proposing to your principal that the district bring your high school up to the average investment level of all other high schools in the district, not just for hardware, but for software, support and staff training, and curriculum development. Second, recruit other parents with similar concerns, and offer to join with interested teachers to form a technology development working group. Your interest could only help propel the cause further. This group can draft a technology plan that will guide you through all the challenges ahead.

If your group chooses to pursue used hardware, you'll find a number of groups around the state that donate computers to schools. (See the first appendix for a list of reputable nonprofits that can provide used equipment to your school.) The Computer Recycling Centers are well regarded. But keep in mind that what's free today can cost you terribly tomorrow. Repairs and systems integration are the hidden price tag of used equipment, acquired willy-nilly.

One organization that has for ten years matched volunteer computer consultants to schools and nonprofits is CompuMentor. They can do much to reduce the costs of training and support that often receive too little attention. CompuMentor also has a software donation program, recycling donated software from major companies.

Title I

9. *When my older son attended school, he was in a special program for slow learners, which took a special computer class, and went on a four-day science field trip where the class spent time with real scientists. This really turned him around, and he's been interested in school ever since. My daughter is also a slow learner, but she doesn't get any of these special programs. Why not?*

Schools receive special funds to provide "enriched educational opportunities" for low-income, low-achieving students. The largest source of these funds is the federal government program called Title I. Until the 1994 reauthorization of Title I, schools were required to limit the use of these funds to a select group of students (whichever group of students the school considered most in need of extra support). However, in 1994, Congress agreed to allow eligible schools (schools serving low-achieving students from low-income families) to use these funds to support "whole school change efforts"—that is, to enrich the educational program for all students. Schools that apply for Title I funds must ensure that:

- Title I students meet the same educational standards that have been adopted for all students. (In states like California, where standards have not yet been adopted, Title I must be used to ensure that eligible students are taught the same knowledge and skills as all other students, not a watered-down curriculum.)
- They provide increased educational opportunities by offering before- and after-school programs, and summer school.
- At least a portion of these funds are used to provide quality professional development for teachers and others (including parents).
- The entire school community—including parents, teachers, and (in high school) students—is involved in deciding how to use Title I funds.

The 1994 reauthorization re-emphasized school accountability. By 2001, schools receiving Title I funding must demonstrate progress toward improved test scores in reading/language arts and math, or risk losing funds. The definition of this progress is determined at the state level.

If you are concerned about how your school's funds are being used, consider joining your school's Title I advisory committee and/or calling the state group that advises parents about their Title I rights.[11]

Slow-paced Title I

10.   *My son is in an enrichment program for low-achievers funded through Title I. At the rate they're teaching, none of the students will ever learn enough to get a good job or attend college, even if they graduate from high school. Does Title I mean the students can't learn?*

No, definitely not. The program is intended to improve students' skills so that they are achieving at grade level. Unfortunately, school people—teachers, administrators, and others—often expect students from low-income families to have problems learning, so they structure the curriculum and teach to those lower expectations. It's difficult, but you need to change their minds or to find schools and teachers who expect more from these students. There's a significant body of research that argues that slower learners who receive a more accelerated education can achieve at grade level and above.[12]

Title I funds should not only provide an enriched education, they should provide more education. Schools that receive Title I funds must use some of their funds to offer early morning classes, after-school classes, or a summer program. If this extra time is used well, it can help students catch up.

As for organizing, a number of parent groups have organized around this issue. I suggest you contact Community Action for Public Schools (CAPS) for help with information, resources, contacts, and advocacy strategies. (See the first appendix on resources.)

<u>Gifted programs</u>

11. *I don't understand the commotion about the gifted program, and why my sister insists that I find a tutor for my seven-year-old so that he can pass the admissions test. Our school buys every gifted student a new dictionary, and takes them on two field trips a year. Our family can provide that without help from the school. What's the big deal?*

Parents seek the gifted label because it opens doors for their child, now and in the future. Testing for the gifted and talented education program (known as GATE) typically happens in the second grade, although you can request that your child be tested at any time. Once a child has been labeled as gifted, this designation is recorded in his school records and follows him throughout his school career. While being gifted can take various forms, most schools have chosen to define it in terms of intellectual and academic skills.

In 1997, the state significantly increased funding for gifted programs, a trend also reflected in the 1998–99 budget. But even with minimal funding, some schools provided interesting enrichment activities, usually with gifted students attending a special class during the school day or before or after school. Many of these enrichment activities are not experiences that a parent could easily provide on her own. The California Association for the Gifted focuses on helping schools develop educational opportunities for their gifted students. (See the first appendix on resources.)

Training for jobs

> 12. *Vocational education has changed since I went to school, when the only courses were woodworking and auto shop. But I still don't see that it will help my son get a job. I think vocational education is a waste of time if it doesn't lead to employment.*

I agree that vocational education should certainly lead toward a job. But vocational education has changed a lot in just the last few years, partially inspired by the rapid rate of technological innovations and plant closures. In 1994, Congress passed the School-to-Work Opportunity Act (STWOA), funding programs that integrate academics and occupational skills to prepare students for "the real world of work." STWOA programs introduce students to all facets of an industry—the technical and production skills, management, marketing, and so forth. Some programs have also developed volunteer and paid work opportunities, in which students learn by doing.

"It's obvious that the main emphasis of the schools all over California is to prepare students to meet qualifications for the University of California. But we have very few students who meet those criteria. So we realized the needs of the majority of the students were not being met," explained Lloyd Hokit, a retired educator from Bakersfield College and a member of the planning committee for the Kern County pro-

---

Oakland Health & Bioscience Academy

Operating as a "school within a school," the Oakland Health & Bioscience Academy at Oakland Tech prepares students for careers in health, medicine, life sciences, and biotechnology. Academy students spend up to 80 percent of their day in interrelated academic and lab classes integrated around health and bioscience themes. Students also participate in a variety of related worksite learning, from career exploration to clinical rotations, and summer and senior year internships. The Academy is recognized by educators, community groups, and businesses as "one of the best educational programs in the country" and "a model for replication." Graduates continue their education at the community college, and at four-year colleges and universities. Students who enter the job market immediately after graduation are hired by participating and other local employers.[13]

gram. Kern County's programs stress basic job-readiness skills, and co-operation. In some classrooms, students who demonstrate these skills are "paid" with grades; students who slack off are "docked" for infractions and as compensation must work "overtime" during lunch or after class.

Tracking

13. *I don't believe in tracking, but my son's fifth-grade teacher does. What should I do?*

You should organize a group of like-minded parents to challenge this practice. In the meantime, though, as long as your son is in a classroom where students are tracked into what teachers call "ability groups," I would try to get him into one of the top groups (though many teachers and some parents would not agree). Students who are perceived as successful—by their teachers, families, and peers, and by themselves—often have an easier time in school.

Although skill-level grouping is a common school practice, particularly in subjects where one lesson builds on another (e.g., children need to know their letters before learning to read), decades of research have documented the damaging effects of tracking on both slow learners

> **On the Wrong Track**
>
> Tracking (or ability grouping) continues to be a controversial educational and legal issue. Currently, the harm has been defined by courts primarily in terms of racial segregation. Intelligence and achievement tests, teacher recommendations, and other devices have been put to questionable use in segregating disproportionate numbers of African-American children into low-ability groups that offer little or no chance of advancement into mainstream classes. An ever-growing body of research on ability grouping demonstrates that tracking shows little or no significant increase in achievement for children at any intellectual level. At the same time, it indicates that considerable damage is done to the self-esteem and motivation of children placed in the lower tracks.

and quicker students. Because teachers anticipate that students in the lower tracks will have more problems learning, they often try to protect them by giving them a simplified, watered-down curriculum and limiting the time devoted to academic instruction. On the other hand, students in the top track may suffer from the pressure of being expected always to excel. Students seem to learn best in mixed-level classes, where the faster students have an opportunity to share their knowledge and where the slower students are not humiliated for having problems in learning a particular subject.

The relationship between tracking and racism has figured in several recent lawsuits, including one by parents of Hispanic and other minority students in the San Jose Unified School District. The parents in that case argued that tracking was, in effect, resegregating the schools. The court agreed, and ordered the district to implement desegregated and mixed-ability classes in grades K–9, and to show progress toward desegregation in high school classes.

<u>Discriminatory steering</u>

14. *Because Manuel is good at fixing cars, his high school guidance counselor is advising him to take auto mechanics. Our whole family fixes cars; Manuel doesn't need to go school for this. He's smart. We want him to go to college and study engineering. How do we get the counselor to be on our side?*

Let her know that you have other expectations for your son, and you'd like her to help him realize them. If Manuel plans to go to college, he needs to take the courses that are required for college entry.

Ask the counselor which courses Manuel must take to prepare for entering the engineering track in college, make a list of them, and make sure that he gets into them or any prerequisite classes. If the school continues to place Manuel in non–college prep courses, schedule a meeting with the principal and enlist his support. If the school continues to be resistant, you might want to contact a sympathetic school board member.

I realize you're most concerned about your son, but often equity problems are school- and even district-wide. That means organizing. The Achievement Council has published a helpful and detailed book to help parents organize on issues of equity. I'd contact them for support and information. (See the first appendix on resources.)

Although such extreme steps should not be necessary, parents have filed complaints with the Department of Education's Complaints Management Services and the Office for Civil Rights.[14] Review the appendix on the appeals process. You might also want to call Community Action for Public Schools (CAPS) in Washington for help. CAPS actively monitors vocational programs, assisting parents and attorneys in challenging discriminatory placement.[15]

Sex discrimination

15. *My daughter wants to be an airplane mechanic. Our district has two introductory courses in electrical systems that might be helpful to her. Her counselor has been trying to convince Mary to take courses in cosmetology instead. What should we do?*

Both federal law and the California Education Code prohibit sex discrimination in courses and in counseling. Schools are not allowed to restrict classes to one sex (except physical education), and counselors must provide students with information about nontraditional employment (jobs in fields in which their sex is only minimally represented).

Remind the counselor that Mary's future will be financially easier if she finds work as an airplane mechanic than if she has to rely on the low wages earned by most cosmetologists. Then explain the problem to the principal, and ask that the school schedule workshops featuring men and women in nontraditional jobs so that the students and the school staff can develop a broader perspective on career opportunities. If you know potential speakers, you might volunteer to coordinate these sessions. The legal group Equal Rights Advocates has a hotline you also might call for advice.[16]

If all else fails, you may want to follow the steps suggested in the answer to the previous question.

Single-sex classes

16. *Our middle school had an excellent science course for girls. It brought in women scientists as speakers, organized field trips, even arranged for after-school work experience to convince the girls that science was "cool." The course worked for many of the girls, some of whom went on to major in science in college. Now the school insists that the class be either opened to boys or disbanded. I want my daughter to take this class. What can I do?*

Although many parents, administrators, and teachers persuasively argue the value of single-sex classes, the courts have generally ruled that single-sex programs are illegal, particularly if they are seen as reinforcing old stereotypes or closing doors of opportunity (e.g., auto shop for boys, cosmetology for girls). Programs that challenge these stereotypes are on somewhat firmer ground. Districts have responded by labeling these classes in a gender-neutral way (e.g., "science for the scientifically challenged" or "science with an emphasis on women's contributions") and opening admission to male students who are also math- or science-phobic.

> **Math Phobia**
>
> Three years ago, school officials in the Ventura school district began experimenting with classes for "math-phobic" girls to see if a program that provided extra support could increase the girls' enrollment in higher-level math courses. When the district was sued for offering a single-sex class by parents of boys who also fit the "math-phobic" profile, the district modified its procedures for counseling, registering, and recruiting students for the pilot math classes, to reflect academic need rather than gender.

Bucking the national trend, the State Board of Education has provided funding to districts that want to open "single-gender academies" for middle school students. Districts that have accepted these funds must establish identical all-girls and all-boys schools on the same campus. Initially, six districts were accepted as a pilot project. The effectiveness of these academies will be evaluated at the end of 1999.

Sports programs for girls

17. *Our high school has a pitiful sports program for girls. The teachers are unqualified, the equipment is old and broken, and the girls can use the field only after the boys' teams have finished practicing. I think we could have an excellent basketball team, and some players might even earn athletic scholarships for college. How can I make sure my daughter and her friends have a chance to play?*

While you may be able to make some changes on your own, I'd suggest forming a parents committee to bring this issue to the attention of the principal, your district, and possibly the press. You might also want to file a formal complaint with the California Interscholastic Federation (CIF).[17] Call their office to ask for a copy of their complaint form. Once CIF receives a written complaint, it must initiate an investigation; it will also forward a copy of your complaint to the State Board of Education. Because sex discrimination in school programs, including sports programs, is a violation of federal (as well as state) law, you may also want to file a complaint with the Office for Civil Rights.[18]

It takes a long time to resolve a complaint. In the interim, school officials will probably suggest that your committee focus on raising funds to buy equipment and bring in another coach. While this may be the best temporary solution, it is not an adequate response. The law is quite clear that the sports programs offered boys and girls must be equally challenging and similarly financed. You might suggest that the school promote volunteer efforts to supplement both boys' and girls' programs while it devotes its sports funding to achieving parity between the two programs.

Textbooks

18. *I don't like the social studies texts used in my son's school. What can I do?*

The most direct approach is to discuss your concerns with the teacher. She may be willing to consider other texts—if they are readily available—or she may invite you to lead a class discussion or provide materials that more closely reflect your point of view. You might also consider joining your district's textbook selection committee, by whom these choices are typically made.

The process for selecting textbooks can be very volatile—at every level. Here's how the process works in our state. Approximately every seven years, the state board appoints committees of subject matter and teaching experts (in each subject matter) to review textbooks and to develop a list of approved texts for elementary schools. (As part of the review process, the committee studies the approved current standards and frameworks.) Each committee is required to select at least five separate sets of textbooks for each subject. These texts are then placed on an "adoption list," a list of books that districts may purchase with the instructional materials funds they receive from the state— $29.05 per student in grades K–8, hardly enough to cover the full cost for all the texts and other materials a student uses throughout the year.

Districts may choose from among the five sets of texts identified for each subject matter. But districts are not entirely restricted to purchasing books on the adoption list: up to 30 percent of their materials budget may be spent on books that did not make the list, and, of course, they may also buy books with other funds. In effect, however, most districts limit their purchases to the approved texts.

While high school districts also receive funding each year to purchase textbooks—$19.01 per student in 1997–1998—the state neither evaluates, nor prepares an adoption list for, high school textbooks. High school districts have complete freedom to select their own texts.

Sex education

19. *I don't want my child to take a course in family life. We have very strong personal beliefs, and I do not want her exposed to what the school will teach. May I ask that she be excused?*

Of course. Write a letter to the school explaining why you don't want her in the class. Conflicts with a family's moral convictions, religious training, and beliefs are valid reasons for excusing a child from classes in health, family life, and sex education.[19] At the beginning of each school year, the school district is required to notify parents in writing of all classes that will be discussing topics related to human reproduction, and of the steps parents must take to have their child excused from such a course.

Sex education

20. *I don't think schools should teach sex education, and I certainly don't want my daughter in a class where they're discussing safe sex and handing out condoms. How can I make sure the school doesn't teach this stuff?*

Schools began teaching sex education to older students (students in grades 7–12) in 1991, in response to the increasing number of HIV-infected youth. This required course, which must emphasize abstinence, covers such topics as safe sex, AIDS prevention, and venereal disease. Few high schools—and no elementary or middle schools—distribute condoms; those that do, do not distribute them during class time. At the beginning of each school year, the school is required to let you know when this class is scheduled, what will be taught, and your right to request that your child not attend this class.[20] If you do not want your daughter to attend, you must send a written request to the school asking that she be excused. The school should then excuse your daughter from this program.

School fees

21. *Public education is supposed to be free, yet our school charges a fee for books, fees to rent football pads and other sports equipment, and a fee to ride the school bus. This is fee education, not free education!*

As we all recognize, our schools are sorely underfunded. In school year 1994–95, California spent less per pupil than all but nine other states. Despite a healthy funding increase since then, the additional revenue will probably not be enough to substantially improve California's low ranking. To compensate, schools try other ways to raise funds, through fundraising events and charging fees. However, none of these fundraising efforts, including fees, may be used to prevent a child from attending school.

For many years, schools distinguished between the fees charged to cover instructional materials—books, lab equipment, etc.—and fees for extracurricular activities. While the former have always been banned, the latter were disallowed only in the 1984 *Hartzell v. Connel* decision by the California Supreme Court. In that case, the court ruled that charging fees denies an equal educational opportunity to students whose families cannot afford to pay. In the words of the court, extracurricular activities serve the purposes of "making of good citizens physically, mentally, and morally," just as much as algebra and Latin. This also applies to field trips. A student cannot be denied the opportunity to participate in a field trip because she or her parents cannot pay the fee. Schools organize fundraisers and/or accept partial payment from students who cannot afford the full charge.

Bus transportation is not typically considered integral to education, and thus a bus fee may be charged, with two exceptions: parents of disabled students who could not otherwise attend school do not have to pay a bus fee; and rural school districts may choose to fully fund transportation for students living in remote areas who could not otherwise attend.

When fees are charged, districts must inform parents that they will be waived for families who cannot afford to pay them. Waivers are usually automatic for families on welfare or whose children are in the federal school lunch program. Schools must explain the process for getting these fees waived.

If your school is charging book or other instruction-related fees, complain to the principal or district office, as this practice is illegal. (See the answer to question 3 in this chapter.) Fees for lost or damaged books, however, are not only permitted, but necessary to partly recover the tens of thousands of dollars schools lose in books each year. If you are being charged fees that you cannot pay, the school should let you know how these fees may be waived. If they don't, speak with your principal and the school site council. Families have also turned to the American Civil Liberties Union (ACLU) and legal services for support. (See the first appendix on parent resources.)

2 Assessment

What would school be without tests, and the tension that surrounds them? As a parent you have the right to be informed about the tests your child will take, what they are intended to measure, and how the results will be used. This chapter covers two types of tests—standardized tests and classroom tests—and their impact on the student and the school. Assessment measures used to evaluate placement in special education, bilingual education, and gifted classes are discussed in other sections of this book.

Standardized tests

Standardized testing is a hot topic in education. It's hot at the state level, where the decision was made in 1997 to administer a single standardized test to all students in all public schools throughout the state. It's hot in the principal's office, where a school's evaluation may rest on how well students score on these tests. And it's hot at the dinner table, where parents sit down with their children to see how well they are doing. If parents can decipher the slew of numbers mailed to them by the district or testing service, and if they find their kids scoring about as well as they expected in all subjects, all is usually well. However, if parents find their kids' scores have dropped, they will want explanations. With so many districts mailing test scores within a week of the end of the school year, more skeptical parents have surmised that it is a school tradition to evade parents waving test scores in hand, seeking this form of educational accountability. In brief, the test score is the answer to the parent's core question: "Academically, has my child done okay this year?"

Parent skepticism is fueled by more than just the delayed mailing of test scores. In 1996, the reading and math scores earned by California's fourth-graders were among the lowest in the nation on the National Assessment of Educational Progress, generally considered the most reliable barometer of student achievement. While our eighth-graders did better, their scores were still below the national average in math and science.

Teachers will tell you test scores don't test what they teach; don't measure all students equally well; don't assess creative intelligence; and penalize students who don't know how to take tests, cannot stand the tension of a timed exam, or have a headache or stomachache on exam day and can't concentrate. While all this has an element of truth, standardized tests are one of the few tools the public has with which to hold schools, educators, and students accountable. Getting these test results is the only point in the year when you learn as a parent from someone *other than your child's teachers* whether your child and her classmates are mastering what education experts believe they should be learning.

In this respect, test scores verify two things at once. First, they verify a skill or subject area mastery. Your child is compared to all other students in the national norm group defined by the testing service (always a representative sampling of other kids in other schools in other states at your child's grade level). Thus you learn how your child stands in relation to other students at the same grade level.

Second, the test verifies that what your child's teachers are teaching is covering what the test is assessing. Is your fifth-grader learning decimals, fractions, and equivalents? He should be. He should also have mastered division and multiplication, and dozens of other math skills. A standardized test will let you know if that has occurred. Other than your own review of your child's work, it is your only point of outside confirmation that your child is doing well. My advice: Make the most of it.

Unfortunately, it is not within the scope of this book to offer you a guide to reading these statistical "tea leaves." But some guidance in assessing the general meaning of standardized tests, however brief, is worth offering.

What the scores measure. Your child's scores measure how well he is doing year to year in relation to other students at the same grade level. A score of 80, for example, means that 79 percent of the national norm group scored less well than your child. The score does *not* indicate the percentage of questions answered correctly. Also, if you want to compare your child's scores only to other students at the state, county, district, or school level, you can do that with a little extra effort. Go to either www.schoolwisepress.com for comparisons of school scores within counties, or to the California Department of Education's site at www.cde.ca.gov. To see how your child scored compared to other students at his school, ask your principal to show you these results.

Trends over time. If your child's scores drop more than 10 percentage points from the test given in the prior year, you should ask to meet with your child's teacher. While the scores from different tests can't be compared with scientific accuracy, they can reveal trends that are worth exploring. The Stanford-9 test given in the spring of 1998 will differ from the 1999 version of that test. So even tests of the same name will differ from year to year. But the principle of noting trends year-to-year still applies. All the standardized tests will score your child's test results compared to some national norm group. It is this methodological yardstick—scoring students by comparing them to each other—that makes observing changes in scores year to year well worth doing.

Classroom tests

These are tests designed by your child's teachers. Classroom tests help students, parents, teachers, and schools know what students have learned and what they still need to work on. While these tests should relate more closely than standardized tests to the daily curriculum, most teachers lack the expertise in test design that would enable them to create effective tests.

Sometimes classroom tests take the form of informal quizzes; other times, especially as the child gets older, they are more formal —like midterms or final exams—and cover a longer period of class work. Ideally, teachers use test information to design lessons that better meet the needs of their students. If test results indicate that some students did not understand what was being taught, good teachers realize that they will have to find another way to explain the material. Test results can also help a teacher understand how a particular student learns and the help he might need to master an assignment.

No one test can do it all. Teachers need to use a variety of assessment methods—including observation, project evaluation, and academic assessment—to get an accurate and complete picture of student performance. The school and the teacher need to look at all the information available—not just tests—to form an accurate picture of the child's progress.

Classroom tests are also related to grades. Elementary school students who fail to pass tests may be held back; that is, not allowed to pass on to the next grade level. In high school, students who fail their midterms and finals may not receive credit for the course.

Like test scores, grades matter. To some students, they matter too much; to others, too little. But to you as a parent, they provide further clues to your child's mastery of course content and academic skills.

Several questions in this chapter are intended to help a parent reckon with the fairness of grades assigned. May grades be given for attitude? May they be awarded for any reason other than subject matter competence? Other questions focus on the consequences of low grades, including the most extreme consequence: being held back a year. Still other questions address good grades as a key precondition to a high school student's participation in sports.

Grades and testing are an inescapable part of school life. Like money in the world of work, they are the currency of the student's world. Your efforts to become a school-smart parent will lead you straight into this complicated and controversial subject. There is no path around it.

Questions and Answers

Teaching to the test

1. *For about three weeks every spring the curriculum is set aside so that the teachers can prepare their students for the standardized exam. This year, the school even required students to attend an after-school class to practice taking the exam. I think it's a waste of time. How can I convince the principal?*

Standardized tests are high-stakes tests. In some districts, schools where students' scores are not improving may be closed, teachers transferred, and principals returned to the classroom. Some districts are considering tying salary increases to improved test scores. Others have recalled elected board members when scores do not improve. No wonder your school is doing everything it can to raise test scores! This phenomenon of "teaching to the test" is particularly severe in inner-city schools, where test results consistently point out how poorly students are doing.

This is not a problem you can tackle on your own, and unless you're in a one- or two-school district, I'm not sure that school-level organizing would be effective. Teaching to the test happens because the state, districts, and parents pressure schools to produce good scores. Your parents group will need to convince your school board that these test scores are being used to make decisions they were never designed to make. There are better options for assessing educational progress, and more effective ways to use student and teacher time.

In the interim, I'd ask the school site council to address the issue. There may be some way to integrate the material being covered during those three weeks into the ongoing curriculum. You may even be surprised to discover a sizable group of parents who believe that those three weeks of intensive test preparation were the most valuable instructional time in the school year.

Test scores and school quality

2. *I found a high school I think I want my daughter to attend, but their test scores are not very high. Although the principal seems dynamic, I wonder if I might be making a mistake in requesting that school.*

School and even grade-level test score averages often conceal large differences among the students taking the test. Students who are not yet proficient in the English language may depress the school's average. So avoid concluding too much about a school from its scores without a fuller understanding of the particular students at that school. You might also to review the test scores by class, grade level, and language proficiency.

Visit the school and see what is really going on. It may be a wonderful place and offer just the classes your daughter wants—or the principal may simply be a super saleswoman.

3. *We parents have noticed that all our kids' math scores decline*
   yearly as our kids move from sixth to eighth grade. We suspect that
   our middle school teachers are just weaker at math instruction than
   the math faculty at other schools in the area. How can we use the
   Stanford-9 test score results to make these comparisons properly?

Your hunch can be verified in two ways. Neither of them are purely scientific proofs. But both can provide indicators of the validity of your suspicions. The first approach is limited to results within your school alone. Assemble a history of as many students' math test scores as possible, starting with their fifth grade scores. On graph paper, plot the national percentile rank of each student's score, using fifth grade as the starting point or baseline, and progressing through as many grades as each student has completed. Try to get at least ten students' scores plotted this way. This is a small sample, but one which should give you reason to meet with the principal, and request that she extend your analysis to cover all of the students who have been at this middle school for at least two years. If the trend lines for a majority of the children in your sample point downward, indicating declining scores, you have some evidence to support your hunch.

The second approach requires a comparison of math test scores among middle schools in your district. You'll be comparing results by grade level over at least three years for each school in your district. This assumes that you have at least three middle schools for this comparison, and that they all administered the same standardized tests at the same time of year in each of the prior three years. The more years and schools you can include in your analysis, the better. As with the student analysis above, plot the sixth grade scores of kids in the 1995–96 school year, those students' seventh grade scores in the 1996–97 school year, and their eighth grade scores in the 1997–98 school year. Do the same with the class of the prior year. This will give you two trend lines for each school. If your school's trend lines show a drop while other schools show stable or increasing scores, you have strong clues that the students at other schools are holding their own, while your children aren't faring so well.

Test phobia

4. *My daughter is a terrible test taker. She can't sleep the night before, and even when she knows the material, she can't answer the questions. Short of keeping her home from school the day they administer the standardized test, what can I do? Her teachers grade her on overall performance, so it's less of a problem the rest of the year.*

You could write a letter to the school asking that your daughter be excused from taking any standardized test. A better solution, however, would be to find some way to ease your daughter's tension, particularly if she's going to continue her education or apply for a job where pre-testing is required.

Standardized tests use a very different format than teacher-designed tests. Many schools schedule sessions in which students can practice taking standardized exams. If your school does not, your school council might ask them to begin offering this program. Also ask your daughter's teachers for suggestions (they've watched her take tests) as well as for referrals to "test prep" programs. Finally, reassure your daughter that, although test scores are important, they can never convey everything she knows.

Practice testing is of such acknowledged importance that college entrance exams are taken in stages: the Preliminary Scholastic Aptitude Test (PSAT) is usually administered in the student's junior year, with the full SAT administered a year later. Familiarity with the testing format and the overall trial-run experience often gives students enough confidence to diminish their jitters. The SAT itself may be taken several times, and students' scores generally increase with each taking. Students may then select their highest scores to be sent to prospective colleges and universities.

Golden State Exams

5. *In September, when my daughter entered high school, the school sent parents a notice announcing that all students in the class of*

2000 must take the Golden State Exam. What is it, and what if my child doesn't pass?

The Golden State Exam is not a single exam, but a series of end-of-year exams used to determine the student's knowledge and capability in the core academic areas. While all districts are required to offer the exam, so far, student participation is voluntary. The exams have become quite popular. Student participation has increased from 96,657 in 1987 (the first year of the exam) to 740,250 in 1997—a sevenfold increase. These are demanding tests, and only one in three students earns high honors, honors, or recognition designations on these exams.

Needed: new way to test

6. *My son is bright, but he just doesn't do well on a paper-and-pencil test. Can't the school find another way to evaluate his work?*

Of course it can, if it wants to. Portfolios (see the answer to question 7) are one way. Homework assignments, participation in class, and special projects are other gauges of your child's performance.

Share your concerns with your child's teacher. Let her know you believe that your child knows much more than he demonstrates on paper-and-pencil exams. Ask for her suggestions on other ways to assess his performance, and be willing to offer some of your own. If she says that it's important that your child learn how to take tests, remind her that it's equally important that he be rewarded for what he knows.

Most teachers will be willing to consider your request. If your son's teacher is not, you may want to discuss the issue with the principal. If the principal chooses not to intervene, I'd look for a teacher who uses multiple strategies to assess student learning. You don't want your child to have to repeat this experience for another year.

Portfolios

7. *My daughter attends a good elementary school, but I never hear her talk about taking tests, just putting papers in her portfolio. What's going on?*

Her school apparently relies on portfolios rather than more traditional testing strategies. This method of measuring student progress can have considerable advantages over regular testing, if it's implemented well. In brief, portfolios enable a student to show what they know, with actual work. Teachers who favor this method also like the fact that it measures a wider range of skills and different forms of intelligence than regular, old-fashioned testing. This new way of assessing what students know can also coexist with other, more conventional methods of assessment like pop quizzes and multiple choice tests. So to find the answer to your question, just give your daughter's teacher a call.

When portfolios are used to assess students, they should contain samples of the child's schoolwork, usually gathered over a one-year period, although some schools use multi-year portfolios. Portfolios are intended to provide evidence of learning, revealing how the student learns as well as what she has learned. Your daughter's portfolio should contain not just samples of her best work, but also examples of her work that demonstrate progress over time—successive drafts of a piece of writing, lab notes from science experiments and the completed lab report, or notes from group projects and a copy of the finished product.

The teachers at Ben Franklin Middle School in San Francisco make extensive use of portfolios. At the end of the year, the school schedules a series of assemblies at which students present selected items from their portfolios to share with other students, teachers, administrators, parents, and the public. The portfolios are cumulative, and the final presentation for eighth-graders includes samples from their three years at the school.

If you have questions about the assessment tools used by the teachers in your school, you might suggest that the school schedule an informational meeting for the parents.

Repeating a grade

8. *Because my son is not achieving, his teacher insists that he repeat third grade. What are my rights?*

If your son were in kindergarten, you would have an absolute right to demand that the school promote him. Promotion from other grades, however, is a different matter.

The state legislature has given local school districts the right to develop their own policies and standards for promotion and retention (§48070). Some districts refuse to promote non-achieving students; others believe that repeating a grade is not the best way to master a subject and can cause the student to have social problems and diminished self-esteem. However, whatever the district's policy, schools often honor a parent's persistent request that their elementary-age child not be retained.

The situation changes when the student reaches high-school age. At one time, high schools were forced to admit all students with an eighth-grade certificate; today, however, districts may refuse to accept any student younger than 15 who does not meet their entry criteria. Any student between the ages of 15 and 18 must be admitted to high school regardless of his or her academic achievement.

Retention and its opposite, social promotion—promoting students strictly on the basis of age and attendance—are volatile subjects. Critics of social promotion maintain that promoting a student who has demonstrated that he cannot do the work is setting that child up for failure and loss of self-confidence. Social promotion, they claim, is irresponsible and conveys a lack of concern for the child. Supporters argue that retention has not been demonstrated to increase learning or learning readiness or to improve socialization, and may also lead to diminished self esteem and discipline problems. If a child has had a difficult year, there's not much point in repeating it.

Both sides agree, though, that students who are having problems learning should get academic and other help if they are to succeed in the classroom. For example, in the case of vision or hearing problems, the school can often provide remedial treatments—which may be as simple as moving the student to the front of the classroom. Unfortunately, more complex additional services can be expensive, and although districts are legally obligated to serve these students, it may take persistence on your part to receive these services.

Academic performance and sports

9. *The only reason my son went to school was because he was on the football team. Now, because he does not have a C average,*

he's not allowed to play. I don't know where that rule came from. I only know that John has lost interest in studying and doesn't want to go to school anymore. Why is the school doing this, and what can I do?

Schools have the right to prevent any student who earns below a 2.0 grade average (C) from participating in interscholastic sports, after-school activities, and other special and extracurricular activities. If the school feels that your son will be able to bring up his grades, they may choose instead to place him on one-semester probation, during which time he should be allowed to remain on the team.

This 2.0 grade-point requirement is intended to encourage athletes to study, and to discourage schools from focusing on the athletic ability of star players while neglecting their academic development.

Ask the school if your son may carry fewer courses or less difficult subjects. While schools are generally reluctant to reduce a student's class load—because this translates into reduced funding from the state—they may be willing to make an exception. Make sure, however, that they will allow him to play with this reduced class schedule. Ask that he be assigned teachers who may be able to motivate him to study, and ask the school to help you find a tutor so that John can get back on track and the team.

No warning of failing grade

10. *My son is a freshman in high school. Last semester, he received a failing grade in math because of his "insolent" attitude. That was the first time I heard he was having trouble in math. Math had been Andrew's best subject, and he planned to major in it in college. Now I don't think a math department will consider him. How do we get his grade changed?*

The teacher is the only person who can change a grade, unless it can be proven that the teacher is incompetent, or acted fraudulently or in bad faith, or that there was a mechanical or clerical error. That means you need to request an immediate meeting at which you, Andrew, and his teacher can discuss the grade.

If the teacher refuses to change your son's grade, I suggest that you ask two questions:

- Why didn't the teacher follow the procedures required by the Education Code (§49067) and inform you before the end of the grading period that your son was in danger of failing?
- What are the teacher's suggestions for what your son can do to improve his grade? You should be ready to offer several alternatives for the teacher's consideration, such as extra-credit assignments.

If the teacher still refuses to change the grade, schedule a meeting with the three of you and the principal to discuss the issue. Note that even if the teacher says he will not attend, it is the principal's responsibility to make sure he does. If this meeting is also unsuccessful, insist that the school add your comments to your child's record and that these be included with his transcript. (See chapter 8, "Access to Information: Records.")

Incidentally, I wouldn't worry too much about the effect his first-semester grade in high school math will have on his college choices. The important point is that he should continue to apply himself to the subject and not let this unfortunate incident derail his enthusiasm.

There's no point in continuing a miserable situation. If possible, get your child into another class, and make sure he does well there by monitoring his work and perhaps meeting a few times with the teacher if you have any concerns.

I know of one angry parent in similar circumstances who insisted that the principal schedule a workshop to (a) inform all teachers of the procedures that must be followed before a student can receive a failing grade, (b) formally reprimand teachers who did not follow these procedures, and (c) provide data to the school site council comparing failure rates among teachers and courses.

3 Learning English

When 10-year-old Cam came to the United States, neither he nor his parents spoke English. Because Cam's school did not offer a special program for limited English speakers, he was placed in the regular classroom. At the end of one year, Cam still had trouble understanding his teacher, and could not participate in class.

Raul's mother was angry. Her 11-year-old son had been in bilingual classes for four years, and the school insisted that he was not ready for a regular, mainstream classroom. Raul always spoke English when they were on the street, and he did most of the interpreting for his family. His mother didn't understand the problem.

After two years in a bilingual program, the school believed that 13-year-old Antonio was ready to move into the regular classroom. He had seemed a bright and enthusiastic student in a bilingual class, but he could not keep up with the work in this new setting. By the end of the first year, Antonio had failed half his classes, and both he and the school were counting the days until he could drop out.

Here in California, the 1990s have been a decade marked by language politics and immigration. This has, of course, directly and dramatically affected the way our schools work. In response to the arrival of so many students who were not yet English speakers, educators developed a range of teaching methods designed to teach them English, advance their understanding of core subjects, and—it is hoped—preserve their literacy skills in their first language. These approaches became known as bilingual instruction.

In June 1998, 60 percent of California voters approved an initiative that requires English-learners to be placed in school programs that immerse them in the English language rather than permitting them to be taught school subjects in their native languages. As of this writing, the dust has not yet settled. School districts and others opposing the new law have filed lawsuits. The superintendent of public instruction is just now issuing guidelines to districts still shocked by the voting public's decision to forcibly step into school affairs, and tell educators what to do.

While we Californians are sorting this out, it would serve us well to remind ourselves of the federal laws within whose boundaries we live. It was the 1974 Supreme Court decision in *Lau v. Nichols*, a California case, that alerted schools to their responsibility to limited English proficient students. In the *Lau* case, a group of Chinese-American parents from San Francisco, whose non-English-speaking children spent the entire day in classrooms where all the instruction was in English, argued that although their children attended school, the lack of instruction in their own language effectively denied them an education. In a unanimous decision, the Court supported the parents' concerns:

> There is no equality of treatment merely by providing students with the same facilities, textbooks, teachers and curriculum; for students who do not understand English are effectively foreclosed from any meaningful education. . . . Where inability to speak and understand the English language excludes . . . children from effective partici-pation in the educational program offered by a school district, the district must take affirmative steps to rectify the language deficiency in order to open its instructional program to these students.

The Court's ruling twenty-four years ago helped clarify what schools owed their limited English proficient (LEP) students. And the ruling will help guide educators today as they strain to take apart— and then rebuild—their systems, their teaching methods, and their organization for delivering education to these students who are their customers. Whatever solutions they come up with, they will have to be consistent with the U.S. Supreme Court's ruling in *Lau v. Nichols*.

In this chapter, I hope to provide some guidance to parents whose questions touch on these language-related issues. My travels across the state have given me the benefit of hearing many parents' questions and concerns about learning English, as well as the issues of multicultural coexistence that are so closely related to these language questions. In essence, those questions and concerns are fundamental. The new law only changes the ways in which educators address their customers' concerns.

I have tried to keep in mind the questions faced by parents of English-speaking children, as well as parents of students who are not yet English speakers. As new questions arise, I hope to continue to address them in my capacity as columnist in the web site hosted by School Wise Press (www.schoolwisepress.com). I encourage you to send your questions to me at that address.

Some background knowledge of the facts of supply and demand in the teaching of English are of significance. In brief, California schools face an enormous challenge. The number of students who are limited in their English proficiency has more than doubled in a decade, from 520,000 in 1985 to 1.4 million in 1997. This amounts to one-quarter of all students now attending California public schools. Four out of five of those students speak Spanish as their primary language.

Two reporters for the *Los Angeles Times* wrote about the situation in June 1998.

> As of 1997, California had about one bilingual teacher for every 92 limited-English-speaking students. Most of these teachers were Spanish-speaking, but even for Spanish speakers, the state has just one bilingual teacher for every 77 limited-English-speaking students. In other languages, the shortage grows to ridiculous proportions. For Vietnamese speakers, the ratio is 535 to 1; there are only five certified Khmer-English teacher—a ratio of 4,000 to 1 for the 20,000 limited English students who speak Khmer, the language of Cambodia. The sink-or-swim approach has a long history in American schools. ("Bilingual Classes: A Knotty Issue," Nick Anderson and Amy Pyle, *Los Angeles Times,* 5/18/98.)

Another background fact about teaching English to California students who are new to the language is that one-sixth of those 1.4 million students have been receiving no special support at all. They've been in regular classrooms, unassisted by language development specialists, whether credentialed or not. This hardly seems consistent with the U.S. Supreme Court's *Lau v. Nichols* decision. These neglected students have, in effect, been subjected to a de facto immersion in English. The shortage of qualified instructors is the main culprit here. Let us hope that the reorganization that follows from the new law ends this glaring omission.

Finally, in order to understand the fury of the electorate, it helps to know that students deemed to be limited in their English proficiency were kept in bilingual programs for an average of seven years. In fact, out of California's 8,000 schools, close to 1,000 schools advanced none of their limited-English-proficient students to English-proficient status in the 1996–97 school year. For more than half of these schools, it was the second year in a row of complete futility.

It is not surprising that these students were not advancing into a regular classroom. Under the old law, school districts received extra state aid based in part on the number of limited-English students they served, and bilingual teachers earned as much as $5,000 extra per year, reflecting the scarce supply of qualified specialists. While the new law promises to maintain these extra funds, it is not clear whether students who advance to a regular classroom would continue to be counted as limited-English-proficient for purposes of state compensatory education funding.

So how will the new law work? In brief, it replaces the wide variety of prior programs with a single one-year program of sheltered English immersion (i.e., a class taught almost entirely in English but with the curriculum and presentation designed for children who are learning the language). At the end of one year, it is assumed that the child will have a "good working knowledge of English" and will be able to move into an English language mainstream classroom (i.e., a class with students whose native language is English or who have become "reasonably" fluent in it). The new law encourages schools to "mix together in the same classroom English learners from different native-language groups but with the same degree of English fluency."

The law allows only a few exceptions to the above regulations. Schools may provide classes in a language other than English—that is, in the child's primary language—if the child's parent requests a waiver and one of the following happens:

- the child is at least 10 years old, and the principal and teachers agree that learning in another language would be better for the child;
- the child has been in a class using English for at least 30 days, and the principal, teachers, and district superintendent agree that learning in another language would be better for the student;
- the child's test scores indicate that he is already fluent in English

—he scores at or above the state average for his grade level, or at or above the fifth grade level, whichever is lower—and the parent wants him to improve, or at least maintain, fluency in his primary language.

If you are interested in opting your child out of an English immersion class, you will be filing a waiver with your principal. You're aiming for the number 20 here. If 20 or more LEP students in the same grade choose to take their lessons in a language other than English, then the school must provide that program. If there are fewer than 20 students, then the school must let the students go to other schools that have classes in those languages. This, in sum, is the way the waivers work.

The passage of this law was protested by many school districts, educators, teachers, parents, and advocacy and civil rights organizations, all of whom argue that the new law denies LEP students their constitutional right to a comprehensive education, forces schools to rely upon a largely untested method for teaching English, and denies school districts, school staff, and parents the opportunity to decide for themselves what program works best for their children.

Other concerns have been raised. In some districts, particularly those operating under desegregation-related consent decrees, schools have been ordered to provide bilingual programs that "advance the dual goal of acquiring English language proficiency and fostering academic skills in the content areas." Will the new law or the court order prevail? The state's class size reduction program provides additional funds for K–4 classrooms with 20 or fewer students. How will the law affect the effort to reduce class sizes? And what about district waivers? Under the state Board of Education's philosophy of local control of schools, they have been very willing to approve (and renew) waivers for any district that requests one. Will districts receive waivers to establish their own guidelines and programs for English language learners? The board's decision in May 1998 to let districts establish their own bilingual policies certainly indicated their desire to let local boards go their own way.

This is certainly a new set of rules. But this law, like most, allows for some degree of creative navigation. If you proceed with a good road map—a strong working knowledge of the ground rules—and are blessed with a good sense of diplomatic direction, you should be able to find a route to your destination.

Questions and Answers

Is special education or tutoring better?

1. *In June, my Spanish-speaking daughter completed a one-year course designed to teach her English. This September she was placed in the regular fourth-grade classroom, but she just can't keep up. Because our school doesn't have a bilingual program, the principal suggested a special education class where Tarya could get more individual attention. What do you think?*

I doubt that this is the best solution. Classroom teachers may misdiagnose the problem by calling a child with limited English skills learning disabled, mentally retarded, or even severely emotionally disturbed, when the child is simply struggling to understand the teacher and the subject matter. Teachers whose students are still learning English should modify their lessons to meet their students' needs.

But start by visiting her class. Does Tarya's teacher make an extra effort to help her understand the lessons? Does she pair her with fluent students who may have a better understanding of the lesson? Does she make books available in Spanish that cover the same material? Does she supplement English language textbooks with simpler English language materials aimed at students like Tarya that explain the course material? If you think Tarya's teacher is not making these efforts to help your daughter learn, I'd bring up your concerns with the principal, the school site council, and any other parent group at your school.

If Tarya's problem is simply that she's "not up to speed," it's unlikely that the special education teacher has either the training or the inclination to give Tarya the help she needs to catch up with her classmates. Special education teachers are trained to teach students with specific physical, emotional, and learning disabilities; they are not trained to teach English to limited English speakers. So in effect, if Tarya is placed in a special education class, she's not likely to receive the help she needs, and she may be stuck with a permanent label that can close many doors, including the one that leads to college.

Tarya may just need tutoring. Many public schools receive federal and state funds for just this purpose. Districts are required to use these funds to provide tutoring and other support programs "directed to enhancing the pupils' interest and competence in the English language, including extended remedial reading programs, special speech and oral programs, and the teaching of English as a second language."[21]

Less teacher time for English speakers

2. *I am really concerned with what's happening in my son's third-grade classroom. Five students who can barely speak English were placed in his class last month. When John told me that the teacher spends at least an hour a day helping these new students, I visited the class to see whether he was exaggerating. He wasn't. When I was there, the teacher spent well over an hour with the new students, while the regular students were in their seats doing homework. Some of them had trouble and even came to me for help because the teacher had no time. That's not fair. What can we do?*

First, I'd commend John's teacher for being so concerned about the new students. I'd let your son's teacher know that it certainly seemed to you that the "regular" students also needed help. While it's difficult to respond to everyone's needs, some other system must be developed. This problem of how to allocate a teacher's time to children of differing needs is not uncommon in any classroom. The solutions devised by educators include bringing extra aides into the classroom, establishing after-school tutoring for the new students, developing and training parents to volunteer in the classroom, and recruiting teacher interns from a nearby school of education that has a credentialed teacher program.

If the teacher is unwilling to accept your observations, then you need to bring your concerns to another level—to the principal or the school site council—and you need to involve more parents.

By the way, it's good that you were there so that the students could get some help, and, of course, it's possible that they came to you because they wanted to get to know John's mother, or just because they were bored—as you know, it's difficult for eight-year-olds to sit quietly doing homework for an hour.

Parent consent

3. *When school ended last year, my son was just finishing his*
   second year in a bilingual program. Each year I had to give my
   written consent to the placement. This year, the school moved him
   into a regular classroom without even asking me. Is that legal?

It may not be right, but it is legal. Unlike the old law, under which
principals were required to obtain a parent's permission to place their
child in a bilingual class, the new law requires neither parent notification nor parent consent. The placement decision is solely in the
school's hands. But the law does not prevent districts and schools from
actively informing parents of their options. Here's where a parent-
friendly school district could take the initiative to improve their
"customer relations." In my opinion, parents should be given an explanation of the new law, the services their children will receive, the
alternative language learning programs, and the process for filing a
waiver. Your options expand if you use the waiver, which is the formal
way of requesting that the principal allow your son to return to a bilingual classroom. (See questions 10 and 11 for more information on
waivers.) I suggest you take your concerns to the district level, where
you may encounter other parents with similar concerns.

Determining when a student
needs English language instruction

4. *How does a school decide that a student needs an English*
   language program in the first place?

We can assume that school districts will continue to administer
one of several standardized tests designed to measure a student's ability to read and write. These tests usually also test vocabulary comprehension, language mechanics (grammar), and spelling. Students are
scored on this test in a manner that compares them to all other students at the same grade level who took the test. It is worth noting that
the score on a norm-referenced test does not reveal what degree of
skill a student has attained.

But we can't assume how districts will interpret the scores—or
what score a student must earn to place out of an English language

program. The new law's lack of particulars here continues to give districts a great deal of room to design their own definition or standard for English language fluency.

The California school board has always allowed school districts to develop their own criteria for English language fluency. Interestingly, when the Department of Education audited districts to see what standards they used, and how they used them, they found that "45 percent were found in noncompliance with basic initial identification and assessment state law provisions!"[22]

Teacher sued for speaking Spanish

5. *A parent who I've never liked, is suing my son's science teacher because he used Spanish to explain something to the students last week. My son said he and some of his friends needed that explanation in order to understand their chemistry experiment. I can't believe that's not allowed, and that a parent can sue.*

The new law does allow parents to sue teachers, administrators, and school board members for fees and damages if they "willfully and repeatedly" refuse to provide an English language program. That does not mean, however, that the teacher can't ever speak Spanish. The law states that the instruction should be "overwhelmingly" in English. Your son's teacher's speaking Spanish on occasion during class doesn't dilute the obvious fact that the class is conducted "overwhelmingly" in English. However, even if the court throws out this parent's suit, the parent may have succeeded in intimidating the teacher. It would be helpful if you, together with other parents, let your son's teacher know you appreciate what he's doing.

Parents prefer bilingual classes

6. *My 12-year-old daughter is in middle school, and we want her to be in a bilingual program. How do we go about it?*

You need to visit the school and apply for a waiver. This waiver is allowed under the new law and, if approved, would mean the law's requirements are "waived" in your daughter's case for that school year. Your success, however, requires that other parents at your daughter's school and grade level also apply for waivers. Here's how it works.

Schools must provide a bilingual program only if 20 students or more in the same grade apply for waivers. But there's good news here. If your daughter's middle school is like most, and shows an enrollment of about 200 students per grade level, you should have little difficulty finding 19 other parents who want the same thing. The PTA or other parents association might be willing to help you organize this effort.

Spanish language honors class for a Spanish-speaking student

7. *We are Spanish-speaking, and we want our twelfth-grade daughter to take advanced placement Spanish so that she can read our classics in the language in which they were written. The school said she can take the class but she won't receive foreign language credit. Why not?*

Some districts offer credit to students who work to advance their first-language literacy; other districts resist this. My own opinions lead me to disagree strongly with your district's policies. It would be equivalent to denying an English-speaking student who wants to study James Joyce from taking Advanced Placement English because English is his first language. I believe this policy would not hold up well to scrutiny under the light of the U.S. civil rights laws. My recommendation, if you care to challenge your district's policy, is to file a complaint with the Office of Civil Rights of the federal government (see appendix 2). If you'd rather find a lower-profile remedy to this problem, I suggest you speak with the advanced placement teacher, to see if he will oversee your daughter's taking an independent study course, which is an individualized seminar, for honors credit. An innovative teacher might be able to help you avoid a head-on conflict with district policies.

Immersion English

8. *I learned Korean in 26 weeks at the Army's Foreign Language Academy in Monterey. If I can do it in 26 weeks, why can't a six-year-old learn English in a year? In addition, I've read that younger children have an easier time with languages.*

Younger children do indeed have an easier time learning languages than adults, in general. In addition, immersion instruction—

putting someone into a classroom where only the new language is spoken—is a pretty successful way to teach most students. Those of us who
have tried, and failed, to learn a foreign language the old-fashioned
way, in grammar-based instruction, remember how ineffective that
could be. There is little debate here. Where there is great controversy,
however, is over the pace of learning and the lack of flexibility in the
teaching methods proscribed by the new law. The law takes away a
teacher's discretion to offer children the method of language instruction that fits them best. And the law also dictates that the student remain in English immersion instruction for only one year. There is a
considerable body of research that argues for allowing a student to remain in such a program for three years, if needed.

I'd also caution you not to draw too literal a parallel between your
immersion Korean experience and the experience of a young student
learning English while going to school. When you enrolled in that immersion course in Korean, you were already an experienced user of the
English language. In sum, you could already read, write, speak, and understand English in its spoken form. A six-year-old doesn't yet have a
fully formed language base from which to build new language skills.
This makes the child's experience far different from your own. This is
an even more important distinction for a child whose verbal skills and
literacy in his first language are not well developed.

Dual immersion programs
for students who already speak English

9. *I want my six-year-old to be in a dual immersion, English-
   Spanish program. The district refuses to provide it because it says
   that Spanish speakers now need to learn English first. My other
   children did beautifully in that program, and now they're fluent
   in both English and Spanish. Why can't the district continue the
   program?*

The problem is, the only circumstances in which a young (under
ten years of age) English language learner can be placed in anything
other than an intensive English language classroom is when they already know English or require a special education placement. (See chapter introduction for a definition of dual immersion programs.) If your
district is not willing to apply for a waiver to continue this program and

the program is still popular with parents, then the school will have to find some way to supplement the English-only education your children are receiving, perhaps through an after-school program. Outside community agencies may also be interested in providing an after-school enrichment program.

How to file for a waiver for a
child under ten years of age

10. *We've been in the United States for almost two years. Although my nine-year-old did really well in the English language program, she's having a hard time keeping up in math and social studies. The school insists that she just needs more time to catch up. She's really suffering—won't talk at home, and now she doesn't even want to go to school. She was a top student in Costa Rica, so she resents being treated like a poor student now.*

If you're really sure that your daughter's English language skills are at least average for her grade level, and you want her in another program, you should file a waiver and request a transfer to a bilingual program. If her school does not have the bilingual program you want, you may request a transfer to another school in your district or even to a school outside your district. (See the chapter on choosing schools.) Also remember that schools must provide tutoring support for students who have trouble keeping up with their class, and in fact, they receive federal and state funds for these programs. (See question 1.)

Here's how the waivers work. Your daughter can qualify under one of two provisions. First, she can show her mastery of what the law calls "good English language skills, as measured by standardized tests of English vocabulary, comprehension, reading and writing." If she scores at or above the state average for her grade level (the 50th percentile of a state-normed ranking for the fourth grade), she's able to opt out of the mainstream class, and elect to go to a bilingual class. The second way for her to qualify for a waiver is if you convince the school principal and her teacher that she has special "physical, emotional, psychological, or educational needs" that would be better met by another program, then she's also eligible for a waiver.

Obtaining a waiver for a 14-year-old

11. *My 14-year-old is having trouble learning English. She's been in what they call a sheltered English immersion program for nearly a year now, and still hasn't learned enough English to move successfully to the regular ninth-grade program at the high school next September. We would like her to read and write better English before she is expected to compete against students who have spoken English all their lives. What can we do?*

It sounds as though you'd like to keep your daughter in the immersion program, where she's been learning English. You may have some choice to return your daughter to the immersion program, or enter her in a new bilingual program where they're prepared to help students like her. But your ability to realize those choices depends on your filing a waiver, and having it approved. School officials will approve it if you can (a) substantiate that your daughter's English skills are at least at the fifth-grade level, or (b) get the principal and a teacher to recommend this transfer because they believe it will be the best way for her to learn English.

There is a third possibility. You could let your daughter move into the ninth grade program, and see what happens. If she doesn't want to remain there after spending at least 30 school days trying, then you can ask the principal and a teacher who knows her well to consider her what is formally known as a child with "special needs." They simply need to affirm that your daughter would be better served by studying in another program, and award her a waiver.

English skills and high school graduation

12. *My daughter is in high school and I am afraid that her English language skills will hold her back from graduating. Do students need to speak English to graduate from high school?*

Yes, they do. Students must pass an English language proficiency test (in addition to all the required course work) to receive a high school diploma. However, Spanish-speaking students may take the GED (General Equivalency Development) exam in Spanish.[23] Students who pass this exam receive a High School Equivalency Certificate, not quite equivalent to a diploma, but still recognized by employers and colleges.

<u>Why not learn English fast?</u>

13. *When we came to this country, we wanted to learn English, we didn't want to be seen as foreign. Why come here if you're not going to speak the language?*

Most immigrant parents want their children to learn English. The issue is how they'll learn it, and what it will cost the state. Because there are so many variables involved in learning a second language, researchers have not been able to agree on the most effective method for teaching English to immigrant youth. The student's age, learning style, literacy in her own language, and motivation must all be factored into the equation. The teacher's skills, her knowledge of second-language learning, and her relationship with the students must also be considered. Additionally, many parents want their children to be literate in both languages—to be able to speak both English and their "home" language. Schools that ignore the child's home language, they argue, force students to sacrifice literacy in their home tongue for literacy in English.

Florida and California Business Leaders Want Multilingual Employees

While California schools are limiting bilingual education, the Dade County, Florida schools, where about half of the students are Hispanic, have voted to expand bilingual programs. School officials there argued many of the students speak Spanish at home, but are not proficient in reading and writing the language. A report citing the difficulty of local businesses (many of which deal in the global marketplace) in finding bilingual professionals influenced the board's decision.

A California Business Roundtable's report, "Restructuring California Schools," called for bilingualism for all children as a goal of California public education. Like the Miami Chamber, their rationale was California's competitiveness in a global economy. Yet this vision is only occasionally present in the schools.

4 Special Education

"There are no excuses," explained one mother of a special education student. "The district must provide whatever services the child needs. Some services, like physical therapy, are paid for through my insurance, but that is because of the nature of my child's disability. If the insurance didn't pay, then the district must."

This parent is right: all children are entitled to a free, appropriate public education. In the case of students with special needs, "appropriate" public education means special education, a loosely defined term that has evolved over time and continues to mean different things to different people. Currently, about 10 percent of California students receive special educational services.[24]

As recently as three decades ago, special education meant the education of students whose intellect was impaired, perhaps because of an organic brain disorder or a correctable learning disorder. In such cases, school districts were required to customize (hence the word "special") rather expensive methods of educating these children. Prior to that time, "special" students were educated outside the public schools, in segregated classes or in institutions.

Today, the range of students qualifying for special education has broadened considerably, and the services they're entitled to receive have been spelled out far more exactingly. The rights of special education parents have also been expanded significantly.

The pace of change has been swift and the scope far-reaching. The consequences for nondisabled as well as disabled children have sometimes been painful, and the strains on the system—and on the students, parents, and staff working within it—are often severe. This chapter explores these changes, and attempts to address some of the most common concerns of parents of disabled and nondisabled children.

As I have talked with parents of disabled children, I have come to appreciate the range of their worries. Some want their children to be identified as learning disabled; others fight to keep their children from being so identified. Some want districts to educate their children; others want outside specialists to work with them at district expense. Some find the creation of individualized education programs (IEPs) beneficial; others are intimidated by the process, or see unimpressive results.

Then there are the parents of nondisabled children, many of whom are anxious about the time teachers and staff devote to including or integrating disabled students into the regular classroom, formerly referred to as "mainstreaming." They worry about whether their own children's education is being neglected. They raise concerns about classroom disruptions caused by children struggling with learning disabilities, lack of self-control, or emotional problems. Parents fear that some of these disturbances might even threaten the physical safety of their own children.

For all its detractors and inherent difficulties, the inclusion of special education students can present many positive learning and socialization experiences for disabled and nondisabled children alike. It may also benefit parents, all of whom are struggling to create the best educational opportunities for their children in the face of limited or dwindling resources. In striving to accommodate the needs and aspirations of all children, special education inclusion provides everyone with lessons in patience, creativity, tolerance, and understanding. It is also the law of the land.

Another public policy aspect of special education merits special mention: the financial commitment to ensure that a student with special needs receives an education appropriate to his needs in publicly supported programs until his twenty-second birthday or through completion of his prescribed course of study. In this fiscally conservative climate, there's an inescapable conflict for resources between children who are in special education programs and those who aren't. The current cost of educating a special education student is more than twice that of educating a regular student. And although the federal government has mandated—and promised to fund 40 percent of— special education costs, in fact federal funding currently falls far short of that mark. Although special education and inclusion may be discussed in the halls of government in terms of theory or hard numbers, they present difficult daily challenges to teachers and students, and inevitably raise parental concerns.

The scope of this chapter is necessarily brief. I have touched on only the most pressing questions I have heard asked by parents across the state. But the need for information is deep for the parents of disabled and nondisabled children alike. I encourage you to take advantage of the wealth of information available from the advocacy groups and parent information centers listed in the appendix on parent resources.

Before a student can receive special education services, the child's needs and strengths must be assessed and an individualized education program (IEP) must be tailored to meet these needs. The IEP specifies the services the school will offer, the qualifications of the teachers (and others) who will provide them, the learning expected to follow from these services, and the measures that will be used to evaluate student learning.

Parents may object to having their child assessed, to any part of the assessment process, or to the qualifications of the tester. They may also reject all or part of the IEP, or insist upon a reassessment to develop a new IEP and placement. At the other extreme, parents may demand an assessment and services, hiring an independent outside evaluator if the district refuses to conduct an appropriate evaluation. The district must honor the objections and demands advanced by each of these parents, either by agreeing to their request or by trying to convince them of the value of the district's plan. The legislature strongly encourages districts and parents to resolve their differences through voluntary mediation before seeking the services of an attorney.

By law, special education students must be placed in the "least restrictive environment"—that means that they should be in the classroom with non–special education students to the greatest extent possible. For a few students, this means attending one class per week with the "regular" students; other special education students may receive as little as 30 minutes of special instruction per week. One-third of special education students receive what are called "pull-out" services; they leave their classroom for one to several periods a week of special services (e.g., speech classes, occupational and physical therapy, adapted physical education). The other two-thirds receive more intensive support, spending up to half of each school day or even longer with a resource specialist teacher—a credentialed and/or experienced special education teacher who provides academic and other assistance. Relatively few special education students (2.5 percent) have more intensive needs that can only be addressed in special private schools or state-operated residential facilities.

Questions and Answers

<u>Assessment for limited-English-proficient child</u>

1. *I think my daughter needs special education, but she doesn't speak English well enough to be tested, so I'm afraid to ask for an assessment. Do I need to find someone outside the school to test her?*

You may want to look outside the district, but that shouldn't be necessary. All assessments must be provided in your child's primary or home language, and the tests must be appropriate to your child's culture, race, and disability (§56320(6)(3), 56322, 56324). The evaluator (the person who administers these tests) must be trained to use these instruments and be competent in your child's primary language or mode of communication. When necessary, an interpreter must be used.

An assessment for placement in special education must be more than a paper-and-pencil test. Depending on the suspected disability, the tester may observe your child in the classroom, on the playground, and in other social situations. She should also talk with her teachers, and may recommend that your daughter undergo a vision and hearing test, a health screening, and other measures that can help her understand the nature and extent of your daughter's difficulty. She definitely should interview you—as the parent you have a good sense of your daughter's strengths and weaknesses.

If you are not comfortable using English, you have the right to ask that the school provide a translator, both for the interview and when it comes time to develop the IEP (individualized education program),

You can also ask for a free copy of the IEP (translated into your own language, if that would be easier for you).

Assessment for special education

2. *I think my daughter needs special education services. How do I decide what services she needs?*

The school district will help you with that decision. Your responsibility is to make sure that the school (a) fairly assesses your child's need for services, (b) recommends services that you consider appropriate to address these needs, (c) delivers these services, and (d) carefully monitors your daughter's progress and the services being provided in her new placement. The district and family must review the assessment and placement at least once every three years.

If you believe that your child needs special education services, submit a *written* request to the school for a special education assessment. The school has 15 school days to respond. Its response should include both a description of your special education rights and responsibilities, and the district's proposed assessment plan. This response requires your approval. If you would like the school to consider areas that the assessment plan does not address, you have the right to insist that the plan be revised. Except under very limited circumstances, the district cannot proceed without the parent's consent.

I'd also suggest that you contact one of the special education groups listed in the appendix on parent resources to help you through this process.

Who pays for assessment

3. *My daughter has a problem learning. Although the district promised to test her for special education, they kept postponing the test, so I hired a private evaluator. It cost our family about $750 to have her tested. The evaluator agreed that my daughter needed special services and developed a detailed learning plan for us. I want the district to pay for the evaluator's time. Will they?*

They may. When a parent requests an assessment and the district refuses to provide it within 65 school days—15 days to develop the assessment plan and give a copy of the plan to the parent, and 50 days to conduct the assessment and schedule the IEP meetings—the parent may take the child to an outside evaluator and present the bill to the district. However, be advised that the Department of Education generally grants waivers to districts that request extra time.

A parent who is dissatisfied with the evaluation provided by the district, even an evaluation performed in time, may also arrange an outside evaluation. If the recommendations from this evaluation contradict the district's assessment or present information that the district evaluator had not considered, the district must pay for this outside assessment. Districts have also been forced to pay for the attorney the parents hired to argue the case, and for private school placement.

Suspicion of special education

4. *My child is a slow learner, but not that slow. I believe that if he were in a better school he wouldn't be having this trouble. I believe that special education is just another way of not serving black males. I don't want my son assessed, and I don't want him placed in a special education program, but I do want him to receive special services. What can I do?*

Unfortunately, only the label "buys" the service. However, don't give up hope. What you want, and need to argue for, is more thoughtful and appropriate assistance from his regular teacher and from the other support staff.

The first question you should ask the school is whether it has used every possible resource in the regular program to serve your son. By law, schools are required to provide "numerous opportunities" to students who need additional help in mastering the regular curriculum before they can refer the student for a special education assessment.[25] Schools are required to document their efforts to modify the curriculum to meet a student's needs. I suggest that you review this documentation.

Observe your child during class and his interaction with the teacher. Then visit other classes. If you find a teacher whose classroom manner seems more appropriate for your son, request a transfer. Ask his teachers from previous years for their suggestions. Most districts are acutely aware of the disproportionate placement of minority students in special education and are reluctant to force an assessment on a parent whose child does not present a serious behavior problem. If you feel the district is rushing an assessment, resist this pressure until you have determined in your own mind what is best for your child. After all, you know him better than anyone else. Remember, your child cannot be assessed without your formal and written consent, except under some very limited circumstances. If you feel you need help in remaining firm, contact one of the parent training and information centers listed in the appendix on parent resources.

A review of special education data from the Department of Education supports your suspicion. In 1995, African-American students represented 8.8 percent of all public school students but 12.6 percent of all students in special education. This disproportion was particularly evident in three of the four major special education categories: learning disabled (14 percent), emotionally disturbed (25 percent), and mentally retarded (12 percent).[26]

Stuck in special education

5. *My son's third-grade teacher thought he had a learning problem because he was having difficulty learning to read. I initially disagreed with her suggestion that he be tested for special education, but because I was afraid he would be held back I finally consented. The tests indicated that John was learning disabled, and for the past three years he has been with a resource teacher for two hours a day of special instruction. He still can't read any better than he did when he entered the program, plus now he hates school. Any suggestions?*

Step up your advocacy. Review the academic goals promised in John's IEP. Were they achieved? Discuss your concerns with the principal. Ask why a child who was considered barely learning disabled three years ago is now permanently assigned to the special education track. If you can, spend several days in his class. How is reading taught? Who teaches it—the teacher or an aide? How many minutes per day are devoted to reading instruction? How is it taught? You may also want to visit programs in other schools for comparison and for a possible alternative placement.

Then demand that the school reassess John and develop a new IEP. Make it very clear that you expect him to be able to return to the regular classroom full-time within a specified period of time, and that you expect the school to provide the services that will enable him to succeed in this new placement. Let the principal know that you will be closely monitoring the situation.

The learning disabled are the fastest-growing population of special education students in the country. According to a report recently released by the U.S. Department of Education, the percentage of learning disabled youngsters more than doubled from 1977 to 1994. While some children with learning disabilities experience serious learning problems, others receive this label because their teachers are unable or unwilling to modify their teaching methods to accommodate a particular child's learning style. Convinced that the child has innate defects or disorders because he does not respond to her instruction, a teacher may then try to "sell" the parents on this placement by pointing out that the program's smaller classes will enable individualized attention. Sadly, to a parent whose child has received little attention to date, the benefits of an IEP and the promise of smaller classes are very tempting.

Unfortunately, these placements too often do not prepare the student to return to the regular classroom. Immersed in the slower pace of a special education classroom, the child falls further and further behind his peers. The near-total absence of exit criteria from special education programs contributes to this cycle of decreased expectations. Although students labeled as learning disabled are often considered quite capable outside the classroom, the lowered educational expectations make them more likely to drop out of school, and less likely to achieve any but the most basic level of literacy.

Benefits to mainstream children

6. *I can understand what the special education student gains from inclusion in the regular classroom, but what's in it for the regular students?*

They gain an appreciation that children learn and behave differently, that we all have different skills and strengths; a greater acceptance of differences; an expanded view of the world and the varieties of people in it; compassion and an opportunity to be of help to others; and a lessening of the fear that their own behavior will culminate in their exclusion.

When a special education student was placed in my teenage son's class, the interaction between the two of them allowed him to discover a gentleness and patience he didn't know he had, as well as teaching skills that he uses to this day.

More attention paid to special ed needs

7. *I have two children—one in the regular program, the other in special education. It seems to me that the school is more attentive to the demands of special education parents than they are to the demands of parents of regular students, and that only special education parents can hold the school accountable for what their child learns. Am I right?*

In a sense you may be onto something. The IEP certainly represents a more comprehensive and detailed agreement between the parent and the school than do "compacts" or other documents the school provides parents of students in the regular program. (See chapter 6, "Parent Involvement in School Governance.") Because schools must secure parental consent before conducting a special education assessment or completing an IEP, special education laws force educators to be accountable to parents of special education students in ways that are the envy of parents of students in the regular program. The extensive advocacy network supporting parents of special education students and the fear of excessive legal expenditures and fines provide an added incentive for school accountability.

Neglect of mainstream students

8. *A boy from the special education program was recently placed in my daughter's class. I agree that special education students ought to be included in regular classes, but this child is taking up all the teacher's time. Don't regular students have any rights?*

Of course they do. The unfortunate truth is that many classroom teachers have never received the training that would help them develop the sensitivity and skills necessary to work with special education students.[27] (This same lack of training may lead them to recommend children be placed in special education in the first place.)

Returning to a regular classroom from the smaller and more controlled environment of a special education program can be an exciting and frightening experience for a student. This may sometimes be expressed in disruptive behavior. Before the boy was placed in the classroom, the school should have carefully identified the academic and other support it would provide to help him succeed in this setting, including the aide or other services available for the new teacher, and they should be prepared to help him as he makes the transition.

As outsiders you would not have this information; only the child's parent and the teacher (and of course the IEP team) know what was promised. You may want to talk with his parents. You could find that they are also frustrated, and would appreciate your help in holding the district accountable for carrying out the IEP.

While I can appreciate how you might be annoyed with the boy's behavior and the teacher's response to it, as both the child and the teacher become more comfortable these problems may diminish. If they do not, you could request that your daughter be transferred to another classroom. Or, if enough parents complain, the principal may be willing to reassign the boy to a more experienced teacher, or to assign an aide to assist him when he is in the regular classroom.

Support in IEP meeting

9. *I'm getting ready for the second meeting to discuss my son's IEP. I don't like what happened at our previous meeting. Can I bring someone with me to take notes? I'm afraid I'll get confused and forget things.*

Of course you can bring someone with you to take notes; you might even consider bringing someone who knows your child and can help in the development of his IEP. You may also tape the meeting and review it before signing the IEP. If you want to tape the meeting, you must give the district 24 hours notice.

It's possible that you and the district will never agree on all of the services that should be offered your child. If that happens, you can request a reassessment, or you may want to sign those parts of the IEP with which you agree so that your son can start receiving at least some services. By law, the school district must honor your objections and demands. As discussed in the introduction to this chapter, the district may suggest voluntary mediation so that both of you can avoid attorney's fees. Although this can be helpful, you are not required to follow this suggestion.

These rights and others should be included in the "Notice of Parent Rights" the district or county sends parents along with their proposed assessment plan.

The Players

Teachers, Parents, Students, and Principals

5 Educators and Their "Customers"

"I hadn't been at the school more than a week when it became obvious that this one teacher was not doing her job," one principal recounted. "I was visited almost daily by crying, screaming, and cajoling parents who demanded that she be removed from the classroom.

"I had never been involved in the dismissal process, and when I discussed it with my colleagues, they told me not to start it. They said it would only ruin my career." But, the principal explained, "I felt I owed it to the school, and to the other students in the district.

"It took two years of my life. At the end I was spending 40 percent of my time meeting with attorneys and developing documents—and about $80,000 to dismiss her."

What advice does this principal offer others who face the challenge of dismissing a teacher? "You have to be very clear about what you're doing, and you need good legal counsel."

This chapter focuses on hiring, retaining, and firing teachers and principals. (For information on the responsibilities of teachers and principals in relation to specific areas, such as curriculum, discipline, school safety, special education, and bilingual education, please consult those chapters.)

The teacher-student connection is so central to your child's school experience that it is hard to overemphasize. As a kindergarten student, your child will probably be with just one teacher for the entire school year. By high school, he may encounter as many as six or more teachers a semester. Little wonder, then, that when parents have an issue to address with their child's schooling, it is often with the teacher that the discussion begins.

But there is a less visible and, at times, more important player in all this: your principal. Just as the president of a small business subsidiary has the greatest influence in shaping that company's corporate culture, so a principal exerts a powerful influence on the school she runs. Your principal may be so effective at recruiting, motivating, and retaining talented teachers, and at getting rid of poorly performing teachers, that your child may never have a bad teacher. Your principal may be so enterprising in grant-writing and other fundraising that your school has money for great school programs, special equipment, and field trips that other schools entirely lack. Your principal may be so talented at recruiting parent volunteers and incorporating them into the areas most needing attention that you find your school to be better staffed, your buildings better looking, and your library more accessible and better stocked with periodicals than any other in the district.

I believe that parents may at times pay too much attention to the power of district authorities, and too little to the influence of the principal. Do not underestimate the importance of the person who is the boss at your school. Do not be fooled into thinking that because the district calls them "administrators" that this is *all* they do. They lead. They motivate. They manage. They command. They hire. They fire. The right person in this position makes many things possible. The wrong person can block all forms of progress.

Different players have different interests. Teachers and principals have jobs and job rights. Community-elected school boards are at once employers, policymakers, and public servants. Parents and their children are the customers or consumers of the schools and their services. The interests of these three groups often coincide, but conflicts sometimes occur, especially around the rights of students and parents versus the rights of teachers and principals. Other conflicts may arise; for example, between parents, students, and teachers, on the one hand, and the school board, on the other.

When such conflicts occur, you need to know how to find solutions. Who should you turn to? When should you do so? Where can you appeal if you don't find satisfaction? To what extent should you rely on diplomacy, and to what extent on hard legalities? When should you pursue an individual solution, and when will it help your cause to band together with other similarly concerned parents?

Equally important is information about teachers and principals. How do they gain certification? Who decides whether they are qualified to practice their profession? Can teachers teach without earning certification? When is a credential waiver a good idea? What are the pressures on California schools that tend to result in pronounced shortages of teachers? What can a district do to more effectively compete for that small pool of teaching talent?

Here are answers to some of these questions:

The California Commission on Teacher Credentialing is responsible for establishing professional standards for teachers, approving teacher education programs, and issuing teacher credentials.[28] It is also the state agency responsible for issuing waivers that allow school districts to hire applicants who have not completed the requirements for a training credential or to assign credentialed teachers to teach outside their field; for example, an English teacher teaching math.

Although the state is considering alternative routes to credentialing, under the current system, to become credentialed, a prospective teacher must (a) earn an undergraduate degree; (b) complete one year of coursework in a teacher training program, including student teaching; (c) pass the CBEST test of basic skills; and (d) demonstrate subject-matter competence by passing an exam or taking appropriate courses. These requirements apply to experienced teachers from out of state, as well as to beginning teachers. Within five years after receiving the "preliminary credential," the new teacher must complete additional professional coursework for a regular credential.

School districts unable to find candidates holding either a preliminary or clear credential can apply to the Commission on Teacher Credentialing for a waiver to hire a noncredentialed teacher or to assign a credentialed teacher to teach outside his or her field. (Noncredentialed teachers are issued an emergency certificate and are expected to complete their education toward the credential.) Districts hiring a noncredentialed teacher are required to provide the support and assistance that will allow her to function effectively in the classroom—to teach our children.

In school year 1995–96, 13 percent of California teachers (15,153 teachers) were teaching on an emergency permit; that is, they had not satisfied the state's credentialing requirements. Only the District of Columbia and five other states had worse records. The 1996 class size reduction program increased the percentage of noncredentialied teachers assigned to classrooms: Almost 21 percent of the teachers hired in the first year of this program did not have a credential.

Shortages do not affect all districts equally, nor do they affect equally all schools within a district. Urban districts, which tend to serve students who need more intensive academic support, are more likely to hire noncredentialed teachers—about 40 percent of the teachers they hired under the class size reduction programs were not credentialed. Rural districts also have problems recruiting credentialed teachers. Not all fields are similarly affected. Some teaching specialties —special education, English-language instruction for limited English speakers, math, science, reading, and elementary education—are significantly understaffed.[29] Thus it is very likely that many children— particularly students from inner-city and rural school districts—will receive some of their instruction from teachers who, by state-established standards, are not considered qualified.

While it seems reasonable, on the face of it, to expect that anyone who teaches children should possess a valid teaching credential, not everyone views it that way. Private schools often hire teachers without credentials, and many charter schools have argued for that right. Some districts prefer to hire professionals whose practical experience and specialized education exceeds the training offered beginning teachers. The real issues are: Who can help your child learn? And, what can parents do to ensure that their school is recruiting and retaining the most effective teachers?

The Commission on Teacher Credentialing also issues the administrative credential. Candidates for principalship must possess a "professional clear (teaching) credential," at least three years of teaching experience, a graduate degree in school administration, and some administrative experience.

Questions and Answers

Burnt-out/worn-out teachers

1. *Our school has several very tired and burnt-out teachers. They were once good teachers, but they seem to have lost it. Is there anything we as parents can do?*

Greater parent involvement can be one way to inspire new energy, but ultimately only the principal can take action. A principal who is serious about improving the school's educational program must spend time in the classroom, observing teachers and helping them to do a better job. Once it is clear from classroom visits what problems need to be corrected, the principal should follow through by talking with the teachers, listening, and making suggestions about how to improve; calling meetings of teachers who need to coordinate with each other; and getting special training for teachers with problems or teachers who want to develop new skills. Some principals delegate this responsibility to other administrators or master teachers.

In Columbus, Ohio and Seattle, Washington, local teachers' unions have lent their support to programs in which senior teachers are designated to mentor colleagues whose classroom performance is considered inadequate. If the teacher fails to improve—which, according to these unions, occurs in about one out of ten cases—the union counsels her to leave the profession. Despite the Columbus and Seattle precedents, peer-assistance and review programs remain hotly contested within local unions.

Incompetent, but tenured

2. *One teacher at our high school allows his class to do whatever it wants. Five years ago, my older son was in his room; now my younger son is. If anything, this teacher has gotten worse. How do we make sure he doesn't return next year?*

The principal is responsible for hiring and firing, and only he can take action. Because it is so very difficult to dismiss a teacher with many years of classroom experience, most principals take action only if a teacher cannot maintain order—for example, when the noise from the classroom disturbs other teachers, or when students are wandering the halls. The fact that a teacher is wasting the students' time by not teaching usually does not seem to provoke action.

If the teacher cannot be motivated to take an interest in what goes on in his class, the principal has three options: counseling the teacher out of the profession; filing a notice of intent to dismiss; or encouraging/arranging a transfer to another school. The last option, referred to as the "dance of the lemons," is the easiest and most frequently used. All it requires is for two principals to agree to exchange unsatisfactory employees and that the teachers agree to the transfer. Of course, the "dance" may not improve the students' educational experience, but it does give the principals some breathing space, and on occasion, teachers do improve.

Visit the classroom; it's important that you know what's actually going on. Schedule a meeting with the teacher so he can tell you what he expects of the students and his goals for the year. If you are still dissatisfied, you need to discuss your concerns with the principal. If possible, bring in some test scores comparing the students in this teacher's class with students from other classes. The principal may even help you compile this information. Don't expect the principal to make any promises (e.g., that she will try to transfer the teacher). Personnel matters must be kept confidential and cannot be shared with parents.

Finally, if you feel that your son will be wasting his time in this class, ask the principal to transfer him to another class. A year is a long time to waste. (Also see the answer to question 1 above, and chapter 9 on choosing schools.)

Grounds for dismissal

3. What does a teacher have to do to be fired?

It's not only what he has to do, but the whole dismissal process that makes it difficult to fire a teacher. The California Education Code lists ten specific causes for dismissal: immoral or unprofessional conduct, dishonesty, unsatisfactory performance, evident unfitness for service, persistent violation of school laws, conviction of a felony or any crime involving moral turpitude, involvement in criminal syndicalism, a physical or mental condition that makes it unfitting for the teacher to associate with children, membership in the Communist Party, and alcoholism or drug abuse (§44932). The first four are the most commonly cited. By insisting that a teacher can only be dismissed for cause, the code protects a teacher who may have angered a parent, or who simply does not get along with the administration or other teachers.

The dismissal process is long and torturous. School board attorneys estimate that the complete dismissal process—appeals, counterappeals, panel hearing, and so on—takes an average of three years at a cost of about $200,000 in legal fees. This does not include the salary paid the teacher during the time his dismissal is being contested. Because of the costs and time involved, and the possibility of losing the dismissal hearing, most districts attempt to "buy out" the contract of an unsatisfactory teacher—that is, give the teacher a lump-sum settlement in return for her agreement to leave the profession.

Keeping a good substitute

4. *My son has a new, first-year teacher, and she's excellent. Most of the other parents think so, too. The problem is that she's new to the district and is filling in for a teacher on maternity leave. We would like to keep her. What can we do to make sure she stays at our school?*

No matter how much the parents, the school, and even the district may value her skills, a new teacher does not have tenure and can be hired only after all tenured teachers have been placed in jobs, even jobs that may be in areas outside the field in which they earned their teaching credential. Tenure is different from credentialing. A teacher—whether a recent college grad or an experienced teacher from out-of-state — acquires tenure only after she has taught in the district for two years. There are only two exceptions to the requirement that districts first hire tenured teachers: (a) a district may hire a new rather than a tenured teacher when the new teacher has skills that are needed to teach a specific course; and (b) a nontenured teacher may be hired first to further the district's compliance with a court order. If the principal cannot find a way to hire the new teacher under either of those exceptions, you can only hope that the district will still have open positions after all the permanent employees have been hired, and that one of these positions will be at your school.

I suggest that you let both the new teacher and the principal know

Two or Three Years' Probation?

California school districts have two years in which to decide if they will grant a probationary teacher permanent status. Much more common is the three-year probationary period required in 33 states. While some professional associations have suggested expanding the probationary period, others advocate a flexible probationary period of one to four years to provide greater job security for exceptional new teachers and experienced out-of-state teachers transferring into the California system. It would also provide an increased time period for promising, but inexperienced staff to improve their teaching skills.

how you feel. Do this as early as you can, so that they have time to act on your request. Creative principals can usually find a way to work around most obstacles, including waiting to declare a vacancy until all tenured teachers have been placed. Of course, your plea will be more effective if the parents' enthusiasm translates into fewer discipline problems, improved test scores, and increased parent involvement. Good luck.

Parents in the hiring process

5. *I think parents should be involved in the interview panel for new teachers. How can I convince our school to open the process to parents?*

You cannot take on the battle alone, and you'll have a difficult time even if others join with you. Parent groups that have advocated greater parent involvement in hiring sometimes succeed in being given a seat on the panel interviewing new teachers. To my knowledge, the wisdom of involving parents in teacher hiring seems to still elude public schools and districts. Charter schools are an exception; there, parents often play a prominent role in teacher selection.

Principal selection is a different issue; parents are often involved in this process.

Doubts about new teachers

6. *We live in a rapidly expanding school district. Over the past three years, our school has hired 17 new teachers. Some of them are very good, but at least five should consider another career. As far as I can tell though, none of them is leaving. What can we as parents do?*

Your parent group needs to make the principal aware of your expectations for teachers. Be specific. Cite examples of good teaching practices you've observed at your school, and contrast them with what you see in these five classes. That means, of course, that you will need to visit classes to develop your criteria for effective teaching. You may want to call some of the groups listed in the appendix on parent resources for their suggestions on what makes a good teacher.

Also, before storming into the principal's office and demanding that she fire the five, stop for a moment and consider their assignments. Because tenured faculty are given first choice of classrooms, new teachers are often assigned the most difficult students. (Principals have also been known to assign teachers they dislike or want to move out of the profession to the most difficult classes.) If these new teachers show promise that they might be more successful with an easier classroom, you need to discuss the principal's assignment process with her. Remind the principal that inappropriate assignments hurt both students and teachers, and insist that she and the staff address this problem.

It is relatively easy for a principal to terminate a new teacher's contract. Due process rights only come into play after tenure has been granted. But principals are responsible for doing more than deciding a new teacher doesn't have what it takes; they are also responsible for helping new teachers to develop their teaching skills. The education code requires that a principal make a minimum of one visit a year to a new teacher's classroom—two visits during the two-year probationary period—and to follow up these visits with suggestions for improvement and additional support to help the teacher do a better job. One visit a year is obviously not sufficient for the five teachers that concern you, nor indeed is it sufficient for most new teachers.

> **Ongoing Training and Support for New Teachers**
>
> Many new teachers have problems maintaining order. Told by their professors that the way to handle unruly students is to simply show understanding and compassion, new teachers complain that they receive virtually no training in discipline, yet it is perhaps the most important issue in their evaluation, and may determine whether or not they continue in the profession.

The California Department of Education, districts, and universities have explored various programs for assisting new teachers in the classroom. The Beginning Teacher Support and Assessment Program (BTSA)—coadministered by the California Department of Education and the California Commission on Teacher Credentialing—is considered one of the more promising. The program assists new teachers in assessing their performance in the classroom, and in identifying meaningful professional development activities that are targeted to their individual needs. Over 90 percent of the beginning teachers who participate in BTSA remain in teaching, as opposed to 65 percent of non-BTSA beginning teachers.

Out-of-field assignments

7. *Many of the teachers in my daughter's high school don't seem to know their subject matter. They're pleasant enough, and they're experienced, so they know how to keep order, but her physics teacher, math teacher, even her world history teacher don't seem competent. My daughter's a senior now, and there's no sense in complaining, but what's going on?*

Since the teachers have been there a while, they must be credentialed. Your school is probably assigning experienced, credentialed teachers to courses they are not prepared to teach, in subject matter outside their own field. This happens far more frequently than it should. A study funded by the U.S. Department of Education concluded that "out-of-field teaching is not simply an emergency condition, but a common practice in the majority of secondary schools in this country."[30]

According to the 1997 study, over 25 percent of all high school students enrolled in math classes are taught by teachers who do not have at least a college minor in mathematics. Of all twelfth-graders enrolled in physical science classes (chemistry, physics, earth science, or space science), 41 percent are taught by teachers without at least a college minor in any of these physical sciences. A stunning 51 percent of all history students are taught by teachers without at least a minor in history. And over four million high school students in the U.S. are taught English by teachers who lack even a college minor in English or any related subject matter. Contrary to the public's perception, "the newly hired are more prone than experienced teachers to be misassigned, and schools with unions have less, not more, out-of-field teaching."

You may not want to confront the principal at this late date, but

"You Cannot Resign," District Tells Teachers

Citing an infrequently used section of the education code, in 1997 the Oakland Unified School District refused to accept resignation letters before the official cut-off date of July 1. Because teachers generally look for work in the spring and schedule interviews during the summer months, Oakland's policy presented problems for school staff. Teachers accused the district of forcing them into involuntary servitude; district administrators, however, disputed that analogy, stating that they are merely trying to fulfill their promise to have all schools fully staffed when classes resume in September.

it would certainly help the next class if you convinced some of their parents to explore your school's teacher assignment process.

No faith in the principal

8. *Many of us believe our principal is no longer competent. Years ago, she was probably adequate. But she isn't today. The teachers don't respect her. She doesn't talk to parents. She can't keep order, even at a school assembly. She hasn't succeeded in getting the district to repair a roof that's been leaking for two years. We need a principal who can motivate teachers, create order among students, and win our fair share of attention from the district's maintenance staff. What can we do?*

Principals are hired by the school board on the superintendent's recommendation, so you'll need to speak with the superintendent. But first, spend some time at the school—observing classes, talking with the students and teachers—and gather substantial evidence of the problems you describe. When you're ready to talk with the superintendent, you need to be very clear about the problems at your school, your expectations of a principal, and your concerns about the current principal's actions. It may take time to effect a change, so you will need to maintain the pressure, and your organizing efforts at the school site. The problems you describe would certainly give a superintendent sufficient grounds to at least investigate further, if not reassign your principal.

In addition, you may find evidence of problems you didn't initially see by reviewing some of the more important school documents:

- the site plan approved by the school site council, which outlines the school's goals (see chapter 6, "Parent Involvement in School Governance");
- the school's most recent self-study and the Program Quality Review Report of Findings (usually conducted every three years);
- recent test scores from standardized tests; and
- the School Accountability Report Card (SARC).

These are all public documents, available at both your school and the district office. If there are also problems in the form of declining student performance, you should find some evidence by reviewing three years of test score data.

9. *The superintendent plans to reassign our principal. We think she's really improved the atmosphere at the school and we want her to stay. What can we do?*

I sympathize with you. The principal is the educational leader of the school. A good principal is constantly pushing, inspiring, hoping, helping, finding a way to get things done. An ineffective principal can destroy a school.

In similar situations, parents have organized phone calls and letter-writing campaigns, used the press, made presentations at school board meetings, and demonstrated. Sometimes this works, and the principal is retained. These tactics are most likely to be effective when the school's achievement scores are rising, and the principal already enjoys the support of the superintendent and school board.

Losing a principal and teachers

10. *We will be getting a new principal next year, and are currently interviewing replacements. While we are sad to lose our current principal, we are even more concerned that some of the experienced teachers are planning to leave with him. What can we do to convince them to stay?*

You need to talk with them. The teachers probably feel some anxiety about the impending change. They may fear that the new principal will not support their teaching style or the special programs that have been created over the years. If things have gone well for them under the current principal, they may wonder if they can adjust to a new administrator.

Listen to their concerns. If parents are represented on the interview committee, you might want to ask the teachers how they would like you to present their concerns. Remind the teachers that you value their skills and commitment and want them to stay.

In my experience, a strong school site council with active parent and teacher involvement (see chapter 6, "Parent Involvement in School Governance") is the most effective means of protecting good teachers. If you have a weak council that takes its direction from the principal, now is the time to strengthen it.

In the end, of course, the decision is up to the individual teachers, and some may decide to leave.

Labor agreements and parental input

11. *It seems to me that once the district and the teachers union have reached agreement on working conditions, most of the factors that might make for more effective educational outcomes—such as a longer school year and fewer in-service days—have already been decided. How do parents get involved in this process?*

It depends on how you define involvement. Parents may comment on the proposed terms of the district-union contract during the public session of the school board meeting. Under California law, schools must make the initial bargaining terms available to parents at the district office at least 72 hours before they are discussed by the board and union representatives. (The 72-hour posting time is also required for all items on the school board agenda, and for minutes from the previous meetings. Active parent groups routinely visit the district office to review these items.)

Some districts invite parents to observe the negotiation process but do not allow them to speak. A few school boards actively solicit parent input. San Juan School District board members, for example, attend parent meetings in order to solicit public input prior to developing the district's offer to teachers.

Parent groups are beginning to challenge their exclusion from the negotiation process. The Sacramento parent organization, Community Partners for Educational Excellence (CPEE), argues that agreements reached by the teachers union and district at the bargaining table—especially on such matters as conditions of employment, hiring practices, layoffs and seniority bumping, teacher evaluation, length of the work year, the school calendar, disciplinary policies, and subcontracting—may not translate into the most advantageous learning conditions for students. Moreover, such prior agreements leave little room for school-site decision-making. CPEE maintains that until parents—as advocates for children—are represented in the negotiations, districts will continue to bargain away the students' educational rights.[31]

Both districts and the unions challenge this assertion. District board members argue that as elected officials, they naturally reflect the concerns of the community. The teachers' unions point to a long history of protecting students' educational rights during bargaining sessions, citing contract negotiations in which the unions refused to allow the district to reduce the school year, increase class size, eliminate entire programs and program specialists (such as art, music, and physical education teachers; librarians, psychologists, speech pathologists, and social workers), or otherwise bargain away necessary programs and services.

6 Parent Involvement in School Governance

"The evidence is now beyond dispute . . . When schools work together with families to support learning, children tend to succeed not just in school, but throughout life . . . . When parents are involved in their children's education at home, their children do better in school. When parents are involved at school, their children go farther in school, and the schools they go to are better."[32]

Research and common sense tell us that education will be most successful if it is a team effort that involves both home and school. Although there are some educators and parents who reject that notion, families and schools are increasingly trying to work together. Indeed, parent involvement in schools has become a major ingredient in school reform.

California is a leader in championing parent involvement, and state laws governing schools often require it. What is new in California, and throughout the nation, is that parents are beginning to participate in decision-making in the schools. This chapter primarily focuses on the parents' role in school-level decision-making, or governance.

The school site council (SSC) is the primary vehicle for this participation. It is required in nearly all California public schools.[33] While the state has not specified the site council's size, it has developed guidelines for members. Parents are expected to hold half the seats at the elementary school level; the principal, teachers, and other school staff comprise the other half. High school councils have a different membership: 25 percent parents; 25 percent students; and school staff including the principal, 50 percent. The people they represent must select these representatives; the parents of children currently attending the school must choose the parent representatives.

The state has given local school councils the responsibility of developing and monitoring the school plan, and the budget that accompanies it. These responsibilities to plan and to budget are no small matter. They can get at the very heart of what makes a school work. The power that parents can now exercise in deciding how their own schools work is the real thing. The challenge lies in using that power well, and in order to do so, you need to master the rules of the game.

A school's budget and annual plan addresses the following six areas:

- A clear statement of the school's goals for the next three years.
- A description of the programs and other strategies the school will use to accomplish these goals.
- An analysis of the effectiveness of the current program in improving student achievement.
- A description of how the school plans to allocate funds and provide staff development to support this effort.
- A description of the plan used to monitor the effectiveness of these programs.
- A description of how the school will determine if its program improvement efforts have been successful in achieving its goals.

After the plan has been approved by the majority of council members, it is submitted to the school board for its approval. The education Code states that "A school plan shall not be approved unless it was developed and recommended by the school site council." (§52855)

Although parents' involvement in governance is required by California law, many schools are hesitant to implement it. "There is a tremendous gap between adopting a policy and implementing a policy," cautioned Maria Reyes, a former consultant to the Family and Community Partnerships Office of the California Department of Education.

Creating real involvement is hard work. It means teaching principals how to welcome, recruit, and manage volunteers, among other things. This is *not* something they learn in their education courses. It means teaching teachers how to put parents to work in the classroom, a place that's traditionally been the teachers' turf. It means helping parents develop a greater sense of ownership of their schools and their obligation to the school community. For parents and educators alike, it means approaching problems with a constructive attitude, an open mind to new ideas, and an ability to listen to and learn from one another. It means hard work, patience, and persistence. But it must be done. Our children are not served by having the most influential people in their lives glaring at and accusing one another, locked in hostile confrontation.

Questions and Answers

Keeping up on child's progress

1. *I am really concerned about how my son is doing in school. Can I demand that his teacher call me every day? My hours make it impossible for me to visit the school.*

You could, but there may be better ways for the two of you to communicate. Let the teacher know your concerns; explain that you work during the school day, and ask if he has any suggestions as to how the two of you might keep in touch. Teachers are usually willing to accommodate a parent's request for more frequent communication. Some teachers are willing to schedule an early morning or late afternoon meeting; others rely on e-mail, voice mail, or even a student-delivered daily report home, at least until the child's work has improved. Your son's teacher may suggest one or more of these options or have other suggestions.

I know it is difficult to take time off work, but it helps if you can visit the school during the first week of classes to introduce yourself to the teacher, principal, and counselor (if there is one). Explain that your working hours don't allow you to attend meetings during the day, but that you want to be immediately informed when your child does something exceptional—either good or bad. Ask for copies of the school rules, the school's expectations for students, and an outline of the curriculum. Be sure to take advantage of the various back-to-school nights, open houses, and parent-teacher conferences to enhance communication between you and your son's teacher, and to monitor your child's progress throughout the year.

Let your son know that you've met with his teacher and the principal, and that you will all be working together to ensure that he gets a good education. Ask about his concerns—in the class and in general—and what he feels would make things better for him at school.

School compacts

2.   *My son brought home a family-school compact, which the school insists I sign. It looks like a contract, but is it?*

Family-school compacts are intended to increase the parent's involvement in their child's education and to advance the cause of accountability. Compacts are an agreement between the school and the parent—and in some high schools, the student—on the responsibilities each will assume over the coming year. Some compacts list only the parent's responsibilities; others include the student's, teacher's, and school's responsibilities. Most schools use a uniform compact form. In a very few schools, the compact is individually designed following a meeting of teacher, parent, and student. Whatever form the compact assumes, a signed copy must be placed in the student's file.

Courts have ruled that a document outlining the responsibilities of the parent and school to the child's education may be considered a legal document only in a private school setting. In public schools, however, family-school compacts are more of a statement of intent than a legal document. So you can't get in legal trouble for not keeping up your part of the agreement.

Although only those schools that serve low-income, low-achieving students are required to develop family-school compacts, the state board recommends that all schools develop family-school compacts as a strategy for furthering family-school partnerships and improving student performance, and the Department of Education provides materials to assist schools in developing these compacts.[34]

Notices to parents with limited English

3.   *Everything the school sends home is in English. My English is not very good, and I'm sure I'm missing a lot. What can I do?*

Write a letter to the school and explain that, while you want to be a responsible parent, you cannot read the notices they're sending home. If you have trouble writing this letter, ask someone else to write it for you and just sign your name. Tell the school that you want them to translate these materials into a language you understand, or to notify you some other way. Schools recognize that students are more likely to succeed when their parents are interested and involved. Because so many parents have problems reading the notices sent home, some schools use ethnic radio stations to get their messages out. Others have hired paraprofessionals who speak the parents' language to call or visit parents. You and other parents who speak your language need to resolve this issue with the school.

If 15 percent of the parents of children attending a school speak the same (non-English) language, the school is required by law to translate all school notices into that language (§48985).

Decision-making and advisory committees

4. *I'm confused by all the committee names. What is the difference between the school site council, the bilingual advisory committee, the school advisory committee, the Title I committee, and the PTA? Which ones have real clout?*

The school site council (SSC) is a *decision-making* body with muscle. It really is responsible for planning how the school will use its resources to provide the best possible education for all students. As discussed in the introduction to this chapter, SSCs are required in almost all California public schools. The SSC is responsible for developing the school site plan, a formal document specifying

- the school's one- and three-year goals;
- the activities the school is planning to achieve these goals;
- the budget allocations to support them; and
- an evaluation plan for assessing progress in meeting these goals.

Districts must assist the SSC in carrying out these responsibilities by providing

- test results;
- copies of the curriculum;
- the school's most recent self-study and/or Program Quality Review Report of Findings; and
- the current site school plan and budget, or information on plan writing if the school is preparing its first plan.

SSC members should also receive a copy of the SSC's by-laws, a meeting calendar, and a list of the SSC members and their term lengths. Because the SSC's role is so central to the school's functioning and success, districts typically offer training to SSC members, as well as providing funds for child care, translation services, food, and other reasonable expenses necessary to enable members to carry out their responsibilities.

School advisory committees, such as the Title I Advisory Council and the Bilingual Advisory Council, are just that: advisory. While their advocacy for students may be welcomed and encouraged, they have no decision-making authority. In some schools, these advisory committees have formally relinquished their tasks to the SSC to facilitate planning, a process that must be repeated every two years (§52870).

The PTA (Parent Teacher Association), or in some high schools the PTSA (Parent Teacher Student Association) is a voluntary nonprofit organization. Its parent members are usually very active in the school. While PTA members often serve on the SSC and advisory committees, the PTA does not have a formal role in school decision-making.

Opening up the planning process

5. *Our elementary school does not have an SSC. We receive extra funds for school improvement and for helping low-performing students, so I know we should have one. The principal, with the help of a few teachers, always develops the school plan. At the last minute, some parents are brought in to sign off on it so we won't lose our funding. How can we open up the process?*

You're right: If your school has this extra funding, it must have an SSC. The problem may be that the principal and his cronies have decided that it's easier to get things done without bringing in the rest of the staff and the parents—and for a while, it is. What you need to do depends on the nature of the problem and the resistance you meet.

Start by talking with your school principal. I recommend bringing several other parents with you. Express your concerns; ask him how parents can become SSC members. The larger, more representative, and better informed your group, the more effective you can be.

Request a copy of your school's current plan, the Program Quality Review or PQR (produced every three years), and the School Accountability Report Card (SARC). If the principal refuses your oral request, put it in writing. Remember to keep a copy of this letter for your file. You are asking for public documents, which must be made available to parents. While the school should give you your own copy of the SARC (it's a several-page document produced by the district), they may insist that you read the plan and PQR at the school. If you must read it at school, take as much time as you need to go through it. Be sure to take notes on everything you read.

The three documents contain useful information for evaluating the effectiveness of your school's programs, and eventually for suggesting changes or modifications, where needed. If any of the information is confusing, you may want to talk it over with parent members from your school's or other schools' SSCs, or with school or district staff.

The school site plan is a very long and very technical document, part of the consolidated application for federal and state funding. In addition to the information summarized in the introduction, the plan includes:

- the names of the elected SSC and advisory committee members;
- information on the school's programs, and the number of students in each program;
- budget information, with all expenditures justified in terms of the agreed-upon goals for student improvement, parent involvement, and program development;
- the criteria used to select students for the Title I program;
- a description of the school's programs for students who are not meeting grade-level standards, English-language learners, students in special education, students in the gifted program, and pre-K Title I students; and
- the signatures of the members of the SSC and the chairs of the other advisory committees, teachers, and the principal, assuring that the plan was developed according to state and federal guidelines.

If you think that the plan was developed without adequate parent involvement, you will want to contact some of the parents whose signatures appear in the document to check it out.

The School Accountability Report Card, which must be updated annually (§35256), summarizes the following information:

- number of students in the school
- average class size
- student-staff ratio
- ethnic makeup of the students and staff
- number of teachers teaching outside their subject matter area
- use of qualified substitute teachers
- description of the school's basic program and special programs
- the school's mission and goals
- the curriculum improvement plans
- the students' progress toward meeting these goals
- estimated expenditures per students
- support services
- student scores on standardized achievement tests
- discipline policies
- attendance and drop-out rates
- number of instructional minutes per school year
- the experience of the teaching staff
- condition of the facility

If you have problems getting copies of these two documents from the school, repeat your request in a letter to the district superintendent. Keep a copy of your letter and record your efforts at getting this information. If you do not hear back within five to ten days, mail copies of your letters to the school board and the press. They need to know what your group is doing, and the problems that you are encountering in accessing public information. Although this should inspire a response, if it does not, follow up your request by calling, faxing, and e-mailing the district superintendent, school board, and the press. Schools should not be allowed to keep parents in the dark, or to make them spend days begging for public information.

There are two other people you might want to contact: the district employee in charge of parent requests, and the staff who reviews and compiles school site plans for presentation to the school board (often called the coordinator of federal and state programs). The complaint officer is required to respond to parent complaints in a "timely fashion," which the state defines as within no more than 60 days. The second person, the program coordinator, is required to reject all school site plan applications that are submitted without proper SSC signatures.

As a last resort, your parent group may also want to file a complaint with the Department of Education's Complaints Management Services, describing how parents have been excluded from the process and explaining that your school does not have a functioning SSC.[35] (See Appendix 2 on the appeals process.)

Fear of retaliation

6. *I'm worried that the school will retaliate against my children if I actively protest a school policy.*

Your fear is not unwarranted, but numbers lessen the risk. If enough parents are involved, it's hard to retaliate against everyone's children. This is a matter that would be perfectly relevant to your PTA or parents association. By all means, raise the issue there. If your school doesn't have such an organization in place, your school district certainly does. In addition, the press may be helpful—go public with all incidents. If the local press won't cover you, then your committee has to print and disseminate your own bulletins, or, I suppose, postings on a community web site.

Talk with your children—they need to know what you're doing and why you're doing it. In the end, you'll need to take your cues from them. If your children are uncomfortable, perhaps you should let other parents take the lead. If they are not uncomfortable, you'll be modeling active citizen participation.

Parent volunteers in high schools

7. *My son, who's in high school, certainly doesn't want his mom hanging around the school, but I think parents still have a lot to contribute. Any suggestions?*

Although your child may be uncomfortable initially, over time he may come to accept your presence, or at least that's how it worked for Margie Robles, the parent founder of Los Padres Unidos in Fresno.

Margie reports that at first her son was embarrassed when she started visiting the school to check on their enforcement of the dress code—though his buddies greeted her enthusiastically. When he realized that his friends accepted her, he began to relax and even teased her about hanging out.

Some parents at San Francisco's Lowell High School have found a place for themselves. The 20 or so parents who participate in the VICCI program (Volunteers in Careers and College Information) assist students (and counselors) by providing information on colleges and financial aid.[36] Parents of high school students also volunteer after hours staffing the phone tree, helping with repairs, sponsoring clubs and activities, tutoring, and so on. It really is a matter of where you think you can help, and how your son accepts your presence.

The principal versus the school site council

8. *Our school has barely enough money for the basics, so the principal decided to eliminate the band program. Can he do that?*

Band is not a required course (see chapter 1, "Curriculum and Instruction"), so he is within his rights to eliminate it. But let's consider how that decision was made. The principal is considered the educational leader of the school, but he does not run it alone. Teachers, parents, and students have a voice in these decisions. The SSC is one vehicle for exercising that voice. In one school facing a similar dilemma, the SSC helped the principal reconsider the decision by reminding him that the goals of the school plan advocated a stronger focus on serving "at-risk" students, many of whom participated in the band.

A "home room" for parents

9. *We think parents would be more likely to spend time at school if they had somewhere to go without feeling they were in the way. How can we convince the principal to allow us to have a parent room?*

I appreciate how uncomfortable it is to feel that you're in someone's way. But space is difficult to find these days, particularly in elementary schools that stand to lose funds if they cannot provide classrooms for all those smaller classes (K–3).

Perhaps the principal can help you find a room or an alcove that you can use. An area specifically set aside for parents conveys a sense of welcome. Parents and schools have equipped these areas with parenting information, information on district and community programs, school reports, minutes of district and school council meetings, and other materials that may be useful to parents. If a specially designated room is not possible, some information can be posted on a parents' bulletin board in the school office.

Parents' presence in the schools—and particularly in the classroom, halls, and schoolyards—contributes to better student behavior and helps make classrooms more conducive to learning. Schools report fewer discipline problems when the students know that parents are around and when parents and teachers have an opportunity to develop personal, working relationships.

In 1995, after the Los Angeles Unified School District opened 109 parent centers, Superintendent Sidney Thompson reported a 13 percent increase in overall parent satisfaction with the district's performance. The Department of Education has established a model parent resource center that may help your schoool develop its own center.

Expanding Rights, Expanding Choices

7 Who Gets Schooled

This chapter addresses parents with young children just entering school, as well as parents whose children are on the verge of dropping out.

The first of these transitions is one of life's milestones, and usually cause for celebration, yet parents facing their child's entry into the school system have many understandable concerns. Here, you'll find answers to some common ones.

The second transition is one of life's crises. When your child is failing in school—or threatens to leave—you need to know what's required of your child, and about the many options school systems offer for getting a diploma or equivalency certificate.

Those of you whose children will soon be entering kindergarten may be wondering if your child is ready to be away from home for so much of the day. You may have many unknowns to worry about—who your child's kindergarten teacher will be; whether your child will be able to keep up; whether the class size reduction program means your child's class will meet in a converted teachers' lounge.

With all these concerns, you may want to know a few things you *don't* have to worry about. California schools are required to accept all students between the ages of 5 and 18 (or until the student has earned a high school diploma), regardless of their physical condition or marital or immigration status. While schools have some leeway on what and how they teach, the hours of instruction are strongly circumscribed. The state requires that schools provide a minimum of 180 days of instruction, although up to seven of these days may be used for staff development. The school is generally closed to students on staff development days. The school day must be at least four hours long, except for the very early elementary grades, which are allowed to have a somewhat shorter day.

The obligations placed on school districts are matched by legal obligations on you and your child. In brief, all children in California between the ages of 6 and 18 must go to school, unless they've already earned a high school diploma. While most districts offer a kindergarten program, five-year-olds are not required to attend school. However, any student between the ages of 6 and 18 who does not attend school and who has not graduated is considered a truant. The California Department of Education estimates that over 10 percent of all school-age kids are truant each day, a striking number. Some communities tend to view truancy with such disapproval that they assign police officers to question and pick up students who they find off school grounds (other than at lunch time) during school days.

Finally, this chapter covers drop-outs: students who leave high school voluntarily, voting with their feet. The lack of a high school diploma or its equivalent is a serious barrier to employment and economic independence. While the drop-out rate has significantly decreased from the early 1990s, students who are Latino, African-American, or Native American are still dropping out at a disproportionately high rate. The dimensions of the drop-out problem can be difficult to understand. The California Department of Education estimates that each year, approximately 4 percent of high school students drop out.

But what if we look instead at the flip side of the drop-out question: what percentage of high school freshmen graduate from their high school in four years? The following table answers that question for the graduating class of June 1997, the students who entered high school in September 1993. The answer is 66 percent, giving us a more dramatic view of the drop-out problem.

Ethnic Group	4-Year Graduation Rate (1996–97)
American Indian	62%
Asian-American	88%
Pacific Islander	72%
Filipino	86%
Hispanic/Latino	54%
African-American	55%
White, European American	74%
State average	*66%*

Source: Demographics unit, California Department of Education.

The state's high school enrollment figures by grade level reveal the abruptness of the fall-off in enrollment by grade level in the high school years. This is presented for the 1996–97 academic year.

Grade Level	Enrollment
9th grade	450,820
10th grade	413,725
11th grade	362,404
12th grade	298,669

The questions and answers that follow may help, whether your child is just beginning school or is on the edge of deciding to quit high school. As you'll see, there's certainly more than one way for your child to complete his education.

Questions and Answers

Minimum age for kindergarten

1. *My son is very mature, and he's also quite bright. But the school says that because he won't be five until mid-January, he's too young to enter kindergarten. If we pay to have him take an ability test and he passes, will the school take him?*

If your child turns five years old by December 2, your district must accept him in kindergarten. Because his birthday is in January, he cannot enter school until the following year.

There is some flexibility in the law, however. A school district is allowed to admit a child whose birthday comes after the cut-off date if the district can be convinced that this exception would be in the best interests of the child. However, this act of persuasion will now meet with a new obstacle. Schools have far less flexibility in managing enrollment in this era of class-size reductions. If a classroom enrolls just one student over the threshold of 20 students, that school loses the incentive bonus offered by the state: $800 per student, or $16,000 for a classroom of 20.

<u>Private kindergarten</u>

2. *If our child is too young to enter kindergarten because he won't be five until the end of January, can we send him to a private school for kindergarten, and enroll him in first grade the following September?*

Many parents with children born just after the cut-off date do just that.[37] However, even after your son completes one year in private school, the district may still decide to hold him back from first grade if they believe it will be in his best interest. Or they may decide to place him temporarily in kindergarten, where the teacher can observe his interaction with the other students and his performance in class before agreeing to move him into first grade.

<u>Home schooling</u>

3. *I want to teach my child at home. What's to stop me from doing that?*

You probably have considered all the personal and social issues, so I'll confine my remarks to the state regulations. Although California law is fairly lenient on home schooling, district responses vary from very supportive to actively discouraging. Since district approval is necessary for the most commonly used options, it's important that your district be at least minimally supportive of your effort.

You have four options for schooling your child at home; the first two are the most commonly used.

- Apply to have your home recognized as a private school with five or fewer students. You'll need to fill out a simple affidavit at the school district office. No fee is required. Anyone may teach in a small private school, and you do not need a credential.
- Enroll your child in an independent study program at your public school. The school will want to maintain some form of contact with you and your child—increasingly, this is by computer —and you will be issued school textbooks. Because schools lose the per-pupil state reimbursement for students who are home-schooled, school districts that previously frowned on home schooling are more receptive to this alternative. It allows them to

receive the per-pupil state reimbursement of approximately $5,584 per year (for school year 1997–98).

- Simply do it—educate your own child. This is allowed only if you have a teacher's credential or a private tutor certificate.
- Enroll your child in a private school and follow an independent study program through that school.

An estimated 20,000–80,000 California students are home-schooled. The figure is imprecise because there is no agreed-upon method for determining who is being home-schooled and who is attending a small private school, or enrolled in the school district's independent study program. Some parents choose home schooling because they disapprove of the public school's curriculum; others feel they can do a better job, need their children to stay at home, or are concerned about what their children will be exposed to at school.

The HomeSchool Association of California can help you through the process, including supplying the names of home-schooling families in your community.[38]

Truancy and lost credit

4. My 16-year-old son is very bright, but he's failing high school because he cuts so many classes. The school won't give him any credit even though he does well on his exams. I thought you earned grades based on what you know, not for warming a seat.

High schools consider seat time very important. They generally justify this policy by arguing that the daily lessons and classroom discussions are an important component of the student's educational experience. This argument is advanced even where class time is devoted to completing homework assignments or trying to keep order, or where a succession of substitute teachers has strayed far from the curriculum.

The education code gives school districts the right to adopt a policy relating attendance to course credits.[39] This is evidently what your district, like many other districts, has done. Grades, however, are another issue. Teachers typically allow students to make up missed work when they were out on an excused absence. One student illustrated the discrepancy between grades and credits with this story. "I received an

A in the class because I did the work. But since I was absent for ten days, I received only partial credit, and I'll have to retake the course."

Schedule a meeting with the principal to discuss your concerns. (In larger schools, the assistant principal handles these matters.) As discussed in the answer to question 10 in chapter 2, *if* the school has not previously informed you that your child was in danger of failing, now is the time to ask why they waited to notify you until it was too late to do anything. If the school refuses to change your son's grades, a note must be included in his school file indicating that he failed because of excessive absences. Wait several weeks and then check his file. (See chapter 8, "Access to Information: Records.")

You'll want to ask your son why he has been cutting class. If it is a school-related issue, the school should help you find a solution. If it is a personal issue, you'll probably have to look elsewhere for help. If he continues to cut, you'll have to find another way for him to graduate. Visit other schools and programs in your district to find one that will hold his interest and address his needs, and then apply for a transfer. (See chapter 9, "Choosing Schools.") You might also want to consider an alternative school, continuation high school, independent study, home schooling, the California High School Proficiency Exam or GED (General Education Development) exam, or early enrollment in a community college. In most of these programs, seat time is not a criterion for grades or for receiving credit.

Tying credits to the student's attendance became an even more volatile issue in 1998 with the passage of a law eliminating "excused absences," and with them, the funding districts had until now received for students who brought an excuse from home. Under the new law, students absent from school for any reason are considered unexcused, and the school's funding is reduced to reflect the student's absence. California thus joins the other 49 states in paying schools only for students who are in school.

Suspension for truancy

5. *My son was suspended from school for truancy. This doesn't make much sense to me. Why would a school suspend a child who isn't attending?*

Rewarding a student who does not attend school by preventing him from attending does not make sense to many people, including the legislature.[40] Nonetheless, it happens. Voice your concern to the principal. While you may be able to convince the school to come up with an alternative for your son—schools often can accommodate one parent's demands—undoubtedly this has happened to many other students. I'd bring the issue to the school site council, and the school board. The district needs to develop a more rational response to this problem, such as a continuation high school (see the following question). And be sure to sit down with your son to find out why he has been cutting in the first place.

Continuation high school

6. *The school district suggested that my son attend a continuation school. What is a continuation school?*

A continuation school is a program offered by the school districts for students who are having problems in their regular school. Continuation schools frequently serve students who are about to drop out of school, pregnant teens or teen mothers, or students who are not succeeding in their regular school. These schools usually provide additional support to their students, such as intensive guidance and individualized instruction. While it is more likely that a district will offer a continuation option at the high school level, some districts also have a middle school continuation program. Smaller districts may band together to offer a continuation program, rather than providing their own. In California, approximately 70,000 California students attended continuation schools during the 1996–97 school year.

Saturday School

7. *In our district, students who accumulate three tardies are assigned to Saturday school. My daughter works on Saturday and she can't afford time off from her job. Can the district demand that she take time off from work to attend a Saturday program?*

Not any longer. The California Association of Student Councils is very proud of its role in convincing the legislature to make participation in Saturday schools voluntary.[41] Although districts count attendance at a Saturday (or Sunday) school as being equivalent to five days of class (both in terms of education and the funding received by the district), "attendance at classes conducted on Saturday or Sunday, or both, shall be at the election of the pupil or, in the case of a minor pupil, the parent or guardian." Like most rules, this one has an exception: the local school board may require truants to attend makeup classes one day over the weekend (§37223[c]). The district and your daughter will have to agree on another way for her to make up the missed time.

Continuation high school/habitual truancy

8. *The school district has declared my son a habitual truant and wants to send him to a continuation school. If he won't attend a school that's half a mile from the house, why would they think he might attend one that's clear across the city?*

For some students who have had trouble in their regular school, the continuation school experience (new setting, different teachers, smaller classes, and more individualized instruction) inspires a new interest in education. Though it seems like a long shot, the district is undoubtedly hoping that it will do the same for your son. However, if you have serious doubts, express your concerns.

The school cannot simply declare your son a habitual truant. Prior to taking such a drastic step, they must notify you that he's been cutting classes; this notification usually includes a warning reminding you of your responsibility for his attendance. The district must also make you aware of its alternative programs,[42] and must try to hold at least one conference with you before declaring your son a habitual truant (§48262).

That's step one. Then, before your son may be transferred, the district must send a written notice to your home, outlining the charges and the district's attempts to bring you in for a conference. The written notice must also summarize your due process rights, including your right to request a pre-transfer hearing.

Truancy petitions are usually reviewed by the Student Attendance Review Board (SARB) or by a truancy mediation program under the direction of the county probation department or district attorney.[43] If these interventions do not succeed in resolving the problem, the SARB may refer the student to juvenile court for prosecution, or the parent may be ordered to appear in court and pay a fine. The education code defines a habitual truant as a student who has been truant (absent without valid excuse) or tardy (more than 30 minutes late) without valid excuse at least three times during the school year. Few schools label students this quickly.

Loss of driver's license and other penalties

9. *The school has threatened to take away my son's driver's license if he continues to cut classes. He needs his car for his job. What can we do?*

The same ruling that allows schools to request the court to suspend a student's driver's license for habitual truancy also allows the judge to make an exception for students who need to drive themselves or their parents to work or to medical appointments. Although you've probably gone through this many times in the past, you and the school must help your son understand the importance of school attendance. Some cities have passed daytime curfew laws that make it illegal for students to "loiter, idle, wander, or to aimlessly remain without any visible purpose . . . between the hours of . . . 8:30 A.M. and 1:30 P.M. on days when school is in session." Students picked up under a curfew law can be charged for violating the law, and they or their parent may be liable for the costs involved in detaining and transporting the student to school, probation, or court. The Los Angeles Unified School District conducted a survey of 118 schools several months into the implementation of a daytime curfew program, and found a 2 to 3 percent increase in attendance and a significant decline in daytime crime, although these figures are being contested.[44]

Many California cities have developed such ordinances and policies.[45] Monrovia reports a 57 percent reduction in its school district's drop-out rate after the city's adoption of a daytime curfew policy.[46]

A youth worker attached to a curfew program explained, "Getting the student into school is just half the problem. Then the schools have to be able to keep them. If they keep on doing the same old stuff, the kids will be back out on the street." This is not news to schools and their supporters, and many schools and districts have applied for funding from the state's Healthy Start program and private foundations to open after-school and weekend enrichment programs that are intended to motivate students to remain in school.[47]

Trying to get back into school

10. *For the past ten months, our church has been tutoring a 15-year-old who dropped out of school. He is now ready to re-enter school, but the school is unwilling to take him because he has so few credits. The assistant principal asked us to find him a GED program. He doesn't want this. How can we convince the school to take him back?*

Schools are required to educate all youths between the ages of 6 and 18, so the law is on your side. Before talking with an attorney, however, I'd discuss the issue with other youth-serving agencies.[48] Counseling and tutoring support programs oriented to "at-risk" youth often enable former truants and dropouts to experience success when they return to school. In addition, many youth agencies have contracted with their school district to allow them to provide credit-bearing courses so that the young person can make up missing school credits.

While the GED can be a viable alternative for students who are old enough to take the exam (a student must be at least 18 to take the GED, although an exception may be made for a 17-year-old who has been out of school for at least six months), and most employers consider the GED equivalent to a high school diploma, it is not an appropriate suggestion for a 15-year-old. For further information on the GED, contact the adult education provider in your county—either the local community college or the high school district.

California High School Proficiency Exam

11. *My child is 15 and ready to drop out of school. Is there any way he could earn an equivalency degree?*

It depends on his age and the grade he's in. He certainly could at 16. Any youngster, 16 years of age or older may take the California High School Proficiency Exam (CHSPE). Younger students may also take the exam if they have completed the tenth grade or are presently in the second semester of tenth grade. Students who pass the exam receive a Certificate of Proficiency, which is considered generally equivalent to a high school diploma, with two exceptions: the Student Aid Commission does not accept the CHSPE for purposes of obtaining a California Grant, as students leaving school early do not always establish a complete grade-point average; and the military does not always consider the CHSPE equivalent to a high school diploma. For further information, contact California Proficiency Testing.[49]

Dropouts go on to college

12. *While I don't think my 16-year old will ever graduate from high school, I think he'll do well in college. Does he need a high school diploma to enter the community college?*

No, he does not. All that's necessary is for the community college to accept him. He does not need a diploma or certificate (GED or CHPSE). Before a community college will accept a student under 18 who still attends high school, the college may require a letter of approval from the high school district. (This has to do with funding: the community college will receive the funds the high school would otherwise receive for educating your child.) An underage student who has already dropped out of school may directly petition the community college for admission.[50] Some community colleges will agree to admit a non-public-school-attending underage student, while others will not. Each community college is given the freedom to develop its own policy. All community colleges will accept older adults who have not graduated from high school.

8 Access to Information: Records

Jack, a special education student, had just been moved from special education and into the regular program (or to use the school's language, he had been integrated into mainstream classes). Although his family was initially pleased with Jack's promotion, they became increasingly concerned when his new teacher would not allow Jack to participate in group activities.

Before meeting with the teacher, Jack's mother scheduled an appointment to review his file. One of the papers in the file was a note from a previous teacher: "Jack is disruptive. He throws crayons in class."

Jack's mother immediately requested a meeting with the principal, his current teacher, and the teacher who had written the note. During this meeting, Jack's former teacher explained that the note referred to his behavior on only one morning. She further added that she considered Jack to be a cooperative student who related well to other children. The new teacher realized her mistake and agreed to begin including Jack in class activities. Everyone attending the meeting also agreed that these remarks would be removed from Jack's file.

Your child's file is a record of his school history. Teachers, counselors, or district staff view these records before recommending placement and other decisions. Prior to 1974, the only people who could read your child's file were school employees. Neither parents nor students were ever allowed to review this information. This changed, however, with the passage of the Buckley Amendment, also known as the Family Educational Rights and Privacy Act (FERPA). For the first time in history, parents were permitted to read the file that the school maintained on their child. Better yet, they were given the right to challenge these records, to add information they considered important, and to decide who, other than the school staff, could read these records.

Soon after the passage of FERPA, California passed legislation bringing its law into essential agreement with the federal law (§49060–49079). Initially, FERPA and the California law only addressed parents' rights in relation to written documents; today they cover all centrally maintained records—written records, and information kept on film, on tape, in computers, or in any other form.

California's records law requires schools to send a yearly notification to parents, informing them of their right to access their child's school records. The notification, which must be in the parent's language and easily understood, should include the following information:

- the types of records maintained by the school;
- the staff person in charge of maintaining these records;
- the process parents must follow to gain access to them and to challenge, correct, add, or remove material from them;
- the charge for copying records; and
- the parent's right to prevent others from reading the records.

Most often this notification is included in the yearly notification of parent rights sent home at the beginning of the school year.

These reforms shift the power balance much more in favor of the student and her parents. But these expanded powers, like all rights, only become powerful when they are exercised. The following questions should provide a useful guide to you when you're ready to act.

Questions and Answers

Information in student's file

1. *What kind of information will I find in my child's records?*

You will find copies of report cards or progress reports; your child's scores on district-wide or standardized tests; test results and evaluations used to assess your child's appropriateness for placement in the gifted program, special education services, or bilingual classes; a record of your child's attendance and medical history; notes from placement hearings and appeals; a list of his extracurricular activities and honors; his discipline record; and what's called the log, a list of everyone other than his teachers or counselors who has requested information from his records, and their reasons for requesting that information. It should also contain your written consent—if in fact you have given it—allowing people other than his teachers or counselors to read his file.

Non-school-related information

2. What about non-school-related information? If my daughter gets into trouble after school hours, will that be in her files too?

It may be. Some schools do place court information in the student's file. However, attorneys with the Department of Education suggest that court documents and medical records be maintained in a sealed envelope in the child's file to restrict access. A teacher reviewing your child's test scores, for example, may not need to read about her after-school problems. Like all school records, these materials are also open to parent review and challenge. A student's file should include only information that could benefit the student's education. If it is not helpful, it does not belong there (see the answer to question 9).

Why review the file?

3. What will I learn from reviewing my child's records? Won't I learn the same things from talking with his teacher?

This is not an either/or situation. Of course it's very important to talk with your child's teacher, but it is also important to review his file, particularly if your child is graduating, transferring to a new district, being considered for special education, or having any kind of school problems. After reviewing the file, request that the school remove, or at least correct, any misleading information (see the answer to question 9). You may also add material that you feel will help new teachers better understand and appreciate your child (e.g., a recommendation from his employer, an award he earned in an outside activity). The only material that belongs in your child's file is information that will help his current teacher help him learn.

Reviewing file before graduation

4. *My son's not going to college, so no one will ever read his file after he graduates. I've gone to school many times to clean up his record—he's been in a lot of trouble. Is there any point in my giving the file one final review?*

Yes, by all means give his file that one last look. Your son may change his mind about college sometime, or an employer might want to read his file. Major business associations, such as the Business Roundtable, National Alliance of Business, and the U.S. Chamber of Commerce, are urging their members to review high school transcripts in making hiring decisions. While this action may be challenged in the courts—particularly if these records are used to discriminate against certain groups of students—it's a good idea for you to review the records one last time so that prospective employers do not receive misleading or irrelevant information.

Requesting a copy of file

5. *It's very difficult for me to get to the school during the day. How else can I review my child's records?*

If you cannot visit during school hours, the school must photocopy your child's records and send them to you. You will probably be asked to complete a written request form, and you may be charged copying fees of no more than 15 cents per page; you cannot be charged for the time staff devoted to copying these records. If you cannot afford to pay the copying fee, the school must provide copies at no cost.

Access by non-custodial parent

6. *My son's mother and I are divorced, and she has custody. Reading his records is one of the best ways I know to keep up with how he's doing in school. Can I do that?*

You can. Both the California and federal record acts extend parental rights to the non-custodial parent. Just go to the school office and identify yourself to the record custodian or front office personnel. If, however, the court has given full custody to your son's mother and she notified the school that they should not release the records to you, you will be denied access.

Access by grandparent or guardian

7. *While I don't have formal custody of my grandchildren, they stay with me most of the time. Lately my grandson has been having trouble in school. When I asked the school to let me look at his records, they refused. I have a letter from my daughter giving me permission to read his file. What can I do?*

Bring the letter with you when you make your request. If they still refuse to let you read his records, your daughter needs to write a letter to the school specifically giving you permission to read your grandchildren's files. The school may insist that your daughter complete a "record-release form" or they may require that she hand-deliver her letter. In either case, after the school receives your daughter's letter, you should have no problem reviewing his file. Keep a copy of her letter for yourself in case any future problems occur.

Grandparents and other family members are not the only people who can inspect a child's records. Some parents want advocates, other educational professionals, or an attorney to review them. This is all legal, and the same authorization process as for relatives should be followed.

Explanation of file contents

8. *I looked at my son's file but couldn't understand half of what was in it. Can I ask someone to explain it to me?*

Definitely. Parents have the right not simply to view the file, but to be given an explanation of everything in it. Ask the record custodian —the staff person who was present when you reviewed the file the first time—to arrange a meeting with someone who will explain the material. If you have problems reading and understanding English, the school must arrange to have a translator with you when you review the files, or to have all of the material translated so that you can read it.

Correcting inaccurate entries

9. *Some of the information in my son's file is inaccurate. What can I do?*

You have the right to challenge any entry that you consider misleading, unsubstantiated, inaccurate, false, or in violation of your child's privacy.

Explain your concerns to the record custodian and request that the material be removed. If she refuses, repeat your explanation and request to the principal. If the principal refuses to honor your request, file a written request with the district superintendent. This complaint must include the name of your child's school, the principal's name and phone number, and your complete address and daytime phone number.

The district superintendent has 30 days to meet with you and the person who entered the faulty information. If the superintendent refuses to change or remove the material, you may appeal to the school board. While you are involved in these appeals, be sure to insist that your written statement describing why you believe the material to be inaccurate be included in your child's file. Remember to keep copies of all your letters and make notes on all of your meetings with the school.

While the school board's decision cannot be appealed to the California Department of Education, an appeal may be filed under federal law. Check with the U.S. Department of Education to determine whether your complaint fits within their guidelines.[51]

Appealing a grade

10. *I wanted to review my son's files because he received a C in biology when we both thought he deserved a B. I thought the teacher might have added some comments that explained the grade, but he didn't. How do I appeal?*

Only a teacher can change a student's grade, unless the parent or student can prove that there was a clerical or mechanical error, the grade was given in bad faith, or the teacher was incompetent. Before any grade can be changed, the teacher must have an opportunity to explain—orally or in writing—why the grade was given. The teacher must also be included in all discussions related to the grade.

Ask the record custodian to schedule a meeting with the teacher, you, and your son. If you are unable to change the teacher's mind, schedule a second meeting with the three of you and the principal. If you are still dissatisfied, you may want to appeal to the district superintendent and even to the school board. In the meantime, write a statement explaining your position and insist that the school include it in your child's file.

Parent information in the student's file

11. *One item in my son's file had nothing to do with him. Instead, it reported on a parent meeting I organized to protest a teacher who had been fired! I was shocked. Does that happen often?*

Less often than it used to. This is both improper and illegal. Most schools conscientiously remove inflammatory material, and material that does not directly apply to the student, from the student's file. Follow the same complaint procedure described in the answer to question 9. I'm almost certain the school will be so embarrassed when you point the item out, that they'll remove it immediately.

Confidentiality

12. *I believe that a program aide in the after-school program my daughter attends has read her file. What can I do?*

Your child's file should include a log of any person, agency, or organization (other than his teachers or counselors) receiving information from her file and their reasons for requesting the information. It should also contain your written consent—if in fact you have given it—allowing people not affiliated with the school to read her file. (There is one exception: Schools may release student records to the court without the parent's consent, although the school must make a "reasonable" effort to notify the parent.)

Sometimes, however, schools get a little sloppy and leave file drawers unlocked, or they allow agencies who are working with your child to read the file without first asking the parent's permission. If you think this might be the case, talk to the principal. If you are not satisfied with his response, appeal directly to the superintendent of your school district. You might also appeal as described in the answer to question 9.

Release of "directory information"

13. We're receiving all sorts of mail addressed "To the parents of . . ." Who gave them our address?

Unless a parent protests, or the school has passed a policy against releasing information to outsiders, schools may release what's known as "directory information" to employers, potential employers, the media, private schools, colleges, and the military. Each school district has the authority to decide what information will be distributed and which groups will receive it. Generally, directory information includes the student's home address, date and place of birth, major field of study, participation in athletic teams, dates of attendance, special awards and degrees, and previous schools attended. In the past, districts also released phone numbers, but in 1991, the legislature recommended that schools "minimize the release of pupil telephone numbers . . . to reduce the possibility of harassment of parents and their families (§49073.5[b])."

Prior to releasing any directory information, the school must let parents know the types of information to be released and the groups that are eligible to receive it. If you do not want the school to release any information on your child, or to release this particular information, you need to send a written request to the school.

When parents request addresses and phone numbers

14. Ten of us are trying to start a parent organization at our school and want to mail some information to all the parents and follow up with a phone call. The school told us that they couldn't release this information to us. Is that true?

Neither federal nor state law prevents a school district from releasing directory information to a parent group. (See question 13 above.) Most districts leave this sort of thing to schools to decide. When your school—the parents, principal, and staff—meets to consider whether to release directory information, they must also decide who is eligible to receive this information, and what information they will release. Address your concerns to the school site council. If you do not have a site council at your school, then you have another set of problems. (See chapter 6, "Parent Involvement in School Governance.")

Your principal or the district may object, claiming that giving you the names and addresses of other parents is a violation of their privacy rights. In this case, you can simply ask the school to include a check-off box on next year's parent contact information form, which states explicitly that the parent gives permission to the school to release the information to parents and other members of the school community.

Who controls files of 18-year-olds?

15. *Tyrone, my 18-year-old, will be graduating from high school this June. When I asked the school to allow me to check his record, the secretary replied, "Ask Tyrone." What's going on?*

On Tyrone's eighteenth birthday, he took over the rights to his own records. Now that Tyrone is 18, you'll need his consent to read his file. Maybe the two of you can read it together. At the very least, you should ask him to review it himself in case there are any inaccuracies or other information that may need to be updated or challenged. Actually, a student does not even have to reach 18 to gain these rights. High school graduates control their own records.

9 Choosing Schools

Much of the national debate about school choice is dominated by two options: charter schools and voucher plans. But in California and 18 other states, legislators have created an exciting and enormously important middle-of-the-road alternative. It is called "limited public-sector choice," and it has been the law of the land here in California since July 1994. In brief, the law frees parents from having to accept a district-assigned neighborhood school. Districts must now allow parents the opportunity to reject an unwanted assigned school and to request an alternative. Although districts are not required to grant the parents' requests, they must take those requests into consideration.

School choice must be made available to parents in all districts with more than one school; however, districts have been given complete freedom to decide how the program will be implemented. The variations are dramatic, ranging from eager implementers who welcome the opportunity to attract parents to the gamut of district schools, to entrenched resisters who, disregarding parental-choice applications, hope to convince parents that their districts, somehow, are not required to participate in this state-mandated program.

A successful school choice program includes a number of factors. Do your schools differ significantly? Can your child travel to school in a reasonable amount of time? Do you have access to the information that makes it possible for you to assess the differences among schools? Do you have access to the schools themselves, so that you can observe classroom teaching, walk through the buildings during school hours, and speak with the principal and some of the teaching staff?

The act of choosing is itself an act that will take you deeper into the world of your child's school. It's a step that may be difficult to take initially. But it's one that will help make you a more school-smart parent.

The competition for students is forcing school staff, and particularly principals, into a new role. Some principals are uncomfortable at having to market their school. One principal lamented, "We were used to people coming to us." Considering the consequences—that principals have to "sell" their schools and district planners have to make allowances for uneven parent demand based on a school's popularity (or lack thereof)—it is no surprise that some districts have avoided informing parents of their expanded options.

Other districts have welcomed the law as a chance to win parents back to the public schools. Capistrano School District and San Jose Unified School District are two examples. They've gone out of their way to publicize news of the various schools' offerings, utilizing newspaper and radio advertising, sending parent teams to shopping centers to pass out flyers, and printing and mailing catalogs in at least two languages highlighting each school's strongest features. San Jose Unified even sends principals out to churches and libraries to recruit students for schools that are under-enrolled.

The parents enjoyed being courted. One mother who attended a house party for a middle school commented, "In this day and age, you just don't get this kind of treatment . . . I feel like [the principal] is accessible, that he will be someone we parents can talk to about our concerns."

This proactive approach to recruiting does much to communicate to parents that they are more than welcome in the schools. It also communicates that they are essential, both at the beginning of the process—enrollment—and throughout the school year.

Some districts follow the letter of the law but not its spirit. They generate little if any publicity to inform parents of their ability to choose; they may even deny that choice exists. The most frequently heard justification for restricting choice is "limited capacity." If all the seats are taken, how can the district allow parents to choose? Indeed, the dilemma is both real and legitimate: crowding is truly a problem. California voters have not approved bonds for new school construction at a pace that matches the growth in enrollment.

The financial rewards for reducing class size in the early elementary grades—$16,000 per class of 20 students—further limits the capacity of already overcrowded schools. The reward allows for no flexibility in enrollment. If a class numbers more than 20 students, the school loses its reward. So one unfortunate consequence of early elementary class size reductions is a considerable restriction of a parents' right to choose schools.

But why can't parents choose among equally crowded schools? What districts fear is that less popular schools would see a net loss in enrollment, while other, more popular schools would see a net gain. Up to a point, such unevenness should be acceptable, and that point is usually specified in the contract the district signs with the teachers union. So if you are a resident of a district that is not implementing a school choice program, probe further—you may well have options.

Here are the particulars of the school choice legislation (or as it is also called, the open enrollment program): "On or before July 1, 1994, the governing board of each school district shall, as a condition for the receipt of school apportionments from the state school fund, adopt rules and regulations establishing a policy of open enrollment within the district for residents of the district" (§35160.5[c][1]) that includes the following elements:

- Parents or guardian may select the school the child shall attend, without regard to the parent's residence, except that school districts retain the right to maintain appropriate racial and ethnic balances among their schools.
- Districts must establish selection criteria for any school that receives more requests than it can serve. Specialized schools with existing entrance criteria may continue to employ those criteria if they are uniformly applied to all students. Other schools must use a random, unbiased process to select students, in which the student's academic or athletic performance is not considered. Priority must be given to students residing within the school's attendance area.
- Districts may make several specific exceptions to their random selection process. Priority may be given to students who can prove that they would be in physical danger, or whose emotional stability would be threatened by attending another school. Priority may also be given to students already attending the school or on the waiting list before July 1, 1994, as well as to siblings of children already in attendance.

The 1994 legislation also addressed choice *between* districts (interdistrict choice). While the district's first obligation is to the students within its own boundaries, districts may agree to accept students from outside their boundaries. Unlike the intradistrict choice program, which is mandatory for all districts, the between-district choice/transfer program is voluntary.

The school choice legislation is rather vague on procedures. By not providing details on implementation, enforcement, and penalties, the law reflects the tension between state-level accountability and local control that has characterized school politics for decades. The letter of the law, however, is perhaps less important than the informal matter of how citizens and school districts work it out. Where citizens expect their districts to create and extend a school choice program, it is far more likely that real choices will become possible.

Good luck in your search.

Questions and Answers

Automatic enrollment
in neighborhood school?

1. *I want my daughter to attend the school down the street from our home. Do I have to apply under the choice program, or may she just go there?*

It depends on how the choice program operates in your district. Some districts automatically place children in their neighborhood school unless the parent requests another assignment; in other districts, every school is open to choice and no space is automatically reserved. Most districts fall somewhere in between these two extremes, maintaining both neighborhood schools and schools that are open to students outside the attendance area.

If your neighborhood school also happens to be an open enrollment choice school, it is important that you make your wishes known, or your daughter may have to attend another school. Talk with the appropriate district staff. Do it soon. The application period may be extremely limited—sometimes as brief as several days—and usually is scheduled sometime between November and May. Don't let this time pass you by.

<u>Choosing a nearby school</u>

2. *I've found a good school for my daughter not too far from our house. How can I make sure she gets in? It's in our district.*

If it's in your neighborhood, your daughter may already be assigned to the school. Check that out with the school or district. If she has not been assigned, ask the district for its open enrollment guidelines, procedures, and forms. Because each district has the freedom to establish its own program, this information varies from district to district. In general, however, both open enrollment and interdistrict choice programs give priority to siblings. Many also favor younger children who attend a child-care facility at or near the school, as well as older students who are in physical or emotional danger at their current school. Once these students have been admitted, a lottery is used to fill the remaining available slots (unless the school has special admission criteria).

If the district denies your application, you'll want to review their appeal process. While it may seem important to focus on the education-related reasons for your request, in fact appeals are usually decided on issues other than academics. Your appeal letter should stress the following types of information:

- Child-care needs—for example, your child attends a child-care program closer to the selected school than to the neighborhood school;
- Medical needs—for example, your child has an illness that requires emergency trips to the doctor and you want her in a school convenient to your workplace so that you can easily pick her up and drive her to her medical treatment;
- Transportation issues—for example, the school you've selected is on a bus line that runs right by your house; or perhaps your child would have to walk one mile to the neighborhood school, whereas you drive right by the selected school on your way to work.

If you have moved or taken a new job closer to the school you selected since you completed the application, be sure to mention that. Although you should already have listed all the priority factors in your initial application—ethnicity, zip code, or a sibling already attending the school—repeat them in your appeal.

Because each school district is responsible for managing its own choice program, the district's decision is final. Neither the county office of education nor the state will hear appeals from parents whose applications have been denied.

Choosing a school across town

3. *I've never heard school choice mentioned, so I don't think our district allows it. I like the school my sister's son attends on the other side of the district. What can I do to have my children go there?*

Although the district may try to discourage parents from exercising choice, by state law, districts with more than one school are required to offer an open enrollment program. This does not mean that all schools are open to all students, but that at least some schools and programs are. Call the district and ask for information on the open enrollment program. If the district denies that there is such a program or refuses to send guidelines, write a formal letter of complaint to your district board of education, explaining that you are prepared to take action unless you immediately receive a copy of its choice guidelines and an application form. If you don't receive this information, you may want to publicly voice your objection at a board of education meeting and/or through the media. As usual, you will increase your chances of success if you can get other parents to join with you.

While some parents have chosen to register their child from another family's address, this is considered both dishonest and a misrepresentation, and hence illegal.

Transfer to "better school"

4. *My son is in third grade, and now that I'm more familiar with the schools in our district, I want to transfer him to a different school. Unfortunately, admission to most of the "better schools" is closed. What can I do?*

All schools have vacancies from time to time. You need to do the same thing you would have done when he was just entering school: go through the open enrollment process. Because the district closes the process (and request list) at the beginning of the school year, in your case persistence may be your best strategy.

The process should not be as difficult as you fear. Let the principal of your preferred school know that you want to transfer your son there. As with any transfer, emphasize any positive reasons for requesting the change—child-care concerns, easier transportation, and convenience to your place of work—rather than your dissatisfaction with your son's present school. Finally, ask that he notify you when a vacancy comes up so that you can quickly call the district office and request the transfer. Although transfers are more easily arranged at the beginning of the school year, you should be willing to accept an opening whenever one arises.

Interdistrict elementary transfer

5. *I work about 25 miles from home and want my 8-year-old son to attend school near where I work. This school is in another district. What do I do?*

An elementary school student is considered a resident of the district in which his parents work and of the district in which they live (§48204[f]) The receiving district may ask you to "get in line" behind the locals. Visit the office of the district near your place of work and try to register your son. Your application should be accepted unless one of these exceptions applies: (a) his transfer would negatively effect either the home district's or the new district's desegregation plan; (b) he is in a special program and the cost of educating him would exceed the state aid the district would receive as a result of the transfer (about $5,584 a year); or (c) either district has already reached its quota of transfer students. The district's decision is final and cannot be appealed (§48204).

However, if your application is denied, you might want to reapply under section 46600 of the California Education Code. This section, which applies to both elementary and high school students, eliminates transfer quotas and the home district's right to reject the parent's appeal. It also permits parents to appeal the district's decision to the county board of education. While this all may seem terribly confusing, what you need to remember is that you do not have to accept the district's initial denial, but may reapply under another section of the code.

While the state does not monitor the interdistrict transfer program, Anne Just at the California Department of Education (phone: (916) 657-2757) can help you through this process.

By the way, once you do win a placement for your child in an elementary school in a district near your workplace, you should not have to reapply. Once a student has transferred into a district, he is usually allowed to continue in that district until he graduates from high school.

If, however, the school in which you are trying to enroll your child is not in the same district as your workplace, despite being close to it (remember, your "district of residence" includes the district in which either parent works), you may have a tough time. Very few districts have designated themselves "districts of choice." So your ability to find a school outside your own district is, in effect, seriously limited by a district's right to opt in or out of this "district of choice" status.

Choices within school of choice

6. *We were able to enroll our daughter in a school with a "health academy" because she wanted to study medicine. After one year at the school, she decided to pull out of that program and just take general courses. It's a good school. Will she be allowed to remain?*

It depends. Students who were accepted into a choice school because they wanted a special program—i.e., they applied to the program and met its requirements—may be forced to transfer back to their home school if they no longer participate in that program. While you wait to hear whether the school will ask her to leave, use the time to consider other school choices, so you will be prepared if need be.

Unhappy with school assignment

7. *It's the first day of school and my son is not going because we did not receive any of our choices, and I don't want to send him to his assigned school. While I want him to go to public school, I don't want him at a school where he'll receive a poor education. What do we do now?*

Education is compulsory for school-age children. You need to get your child into school as quickly as possible. Visit both your district's placement office and the school you want your child to attend, and begin talking. There are usually vacancies at the beginning of the school year because some parents neglected to inform the district that they made other choices. If there aren't any vacancies, enroll him in the best school that will accept him and continue trying to get him into a school of your choice. If there is a waiting list at a particular school, make sure your child is on it so that you may be notified if and when a vacancy occurs and have your son transferred. See also the answer to question 4 above.

Smaller classes, fewer choices

8. *With the new smaller classes in the early grades, our district has threatened to eliminate choice in the elementary grades. What can parents do?*

You and other parents must convince your district that the class size reduction program will be effective only so long as the parents want their children to attend the school to which they have been assigned. If a parent wants her child to attend another school but finds her request denied, she is unlikely to become a satisfied customer of the school district, and far less likely to become a committed and hard-working volunteer in her child's school. Remind the district that the goals underlying school choice—retaining parents who might otherwise leave the public schools, and increasing parental commitment to public education—will be lost if choice is reduced or eliminated.

On a practical level, districts are truly constrained by the unforgiving inflexibility of a 20-student class size cap. Still, a district can take some steps to enable parents to make the most of their freedom to choose. First, they can create a public information system for notifying parents which schools have room in early elementary classrooms. This at least would eliminate the need for parents to scramble for this essential information. Second, districts can take an active role in helping parents "swap" their kids' places, effectively playing matchmaker between parents. Third, districts can do what they call capacity planning differently, taking the preferences of resident parents into consideration. If, six months prior to the start of school, your district surveyed all parents who were intending to enroll their children in kindergarten, and asked them to state their preferred school of choice, think how much more effective they could be in planning for balanced enrollments across all schools.

Who teaches the basics?

9. *I want to send my child to a school that emphasizes the basics. Do districts maintain this kind of information? And if they do, will they share it with parents?*

They do, and it must be shared with parents. Call your district and ask for the information you need. The district PTA or the county office of education might also help. Districts and schools are usually willing to share this type of information, but if you encounter resistance, keep asking until you get what you need. Keep a list of the people you talk with, the letters you write, and the time it takes for your request to be met. Share the steps you had to take to get this information, with both your school board and the media. Insist that the district develop a "parent-friendly" outreach program so those parents may make intelligent choices.

Choosing a school is a major responsibility. The district should help you with that decision.

Racial/ethnic identification

10. *The application form for the open enrollment program asks for our racial/ethnic identification. I know that certain groups have an easier time. Must I tell the truth?*

Only districts under court order or those voluntarily attempting to maintain ethnic balance ask this question. And yes, you must tell the truth. Lying about your ethnicity is a misdemeanor. Parents of multiracial children are allowed to change their child's identity on the school record once during their child's school career. Parenthetically, most families—with the exception of Native Americans and parents of biracial children who decide to change their child's ethnicity of record —are not required to provide proof of their child's ethnicity.

Providing transportation

11. I've found a perfect school for my 9-year-old. The only problem is that it's across the city and I don't know how she'll get there. Our district has a busing program. Will she qualify?

It depends on the bus routes. While the choice law gives you the freedom to turn down the school assignment your district hands you, it leaves with you the responsibility of getting your 9-year-old there yourself. If, however, the bus that goes to the school you prefer happens to come near your home, she should qualify. The only guideline the state has given on this issue is that the district's decision cannot be arbitrary or unreasonable.

Transferring and varsity sports

12. My daughter's passion is sports. Will transferring affect her eligibility for the high school soccer team?

Yes, if it's a varsity team. In terms of eligibility to play varsity sports, the school your daughter enrolled in as a freshman is considered her school, the school she may play for. If she transfers to a different high school, she will be ineligible to participate in varsity sports programs for one year, though she may be able to compete on a lower level.

Breaking rules threatens transfer status

13. After some work on our part, our daughter was finally accepted in a "choice school." Now the school is threatening to return her to her home school because she has trouble getting there on time. Can they do that?

Yes. Students transferred under the choice program must follow the school's rules—which includes arriving on time. Students who are continually tardy or frequently absent, or present excessive disciplinary problems may be transferred back to their home school.

10 Charter Schools

In 1993, California became the second state in the nation to pass legislation that allowed teachers, parents, pupils, and community members to establish and maintain charter schools. "The basic charter concept is simple: Allow a group of teachers or other would-be educators to apply for permission to open a school. Give them dollar for dollar what a public school gets for each student but without any strings attached. Free them from the regulations that cripple learning and stifle innovation at so many public schools."[52]

By May 1998, 133 charter schools were in operation—the majority can be found in northern California. New legislation passed in 1998 promises to greatly expand the number of schools and to liberalize the conditions under which they develop and operate.[53]

The legislation gives charter schools the freedom to develop their own educational goals, courses, teaching methods, assessment measures, calendar, and schedule; they may also hire non-credentialed teachers and are exempt from the state's collective bargaining laws. In return for this freedom, charter schools are held accountable for results—for improving student learning, and increasing learning opportunities for all students, particularly low-achieving students. Parents who are dissatisfied with any aspect of a charter school's program or with their child's performance can withdraw their child from that school. Charter schools are accountable to the legal body that granted their charter—the district, county, or state—which may revoke the charter if the school fails to meet the terms of its petition, "failing to meet or pursue any of the pupil outcomes identified in the charter petition." Charters are granted for five-year renewal terms.

No two charter schools are alike. Each is tailored to the specific needs of the students, the teachers, and the community it serves. Parents who want to play a more significant role in their children's education, teachers, other education professionals, nonprofit organizations, profit-seeking firms, and community organizations have applied for charters. For some, a strong motivation is to escape the terms of collective bargaining agreements and state personnel laws, particularly provisions about selecting employees and evaluating and dismissing them.[54] New schools have been formed; existing public schools converted to charter status; for-profit businesses have been asked to take over the management of a school; and at least one entire district has converted to charter school status.

Most charter schools serve elementary and middle school students; some start small, with only one or two grades, and gradually phase in additional classes. Enrollments in charter schools range from three students to over 1,000. While a few charter schools essentially duplicate the curriculum and teaching methods of their sponsoring district, most have used the freedom to innovate. David Patterson, the Department of Education's Education Program Consultant in the Charter Schools Office, captures the variety of charter schools:

> Some of the innovative approaches and partners that are involved with specific charter schools include the Waldorf approach, partnerships with the Conservation Corps, the Urban League, and county government. There are charter schools that serve expelled students, recover dropouts, and focus on Spanish language acquisition. There are charter schools that place middle school students in work experience settings in the community, incorporate comprehensive family services, use home-study models, are museum-based, emphasize back-to-basics skills, and utilize distance learning [via a computer and modem].[55]

Questions and Answers

Forming a charter school

1. *We are a group of parents and teachers who are considering forming a charter school. Where do we begin?*

You begin by deciding what you want in a school. It's important that you're very clear about this: vaguely stated goals have been the undoing of many schools.

After you have reached some agreement, answer the questions on the charter petition. The petition for charter status requires detailed answers to 13 questions ranging from the school's mission and governance structure to the transfer policy for students and teachers. Because charter schools are public schools, the petition must give assurance that the school will not discriminate in its admission or employment policies, that programs will be nonsectarian, and that tuition will not be charged. Charter petitions must be signed by 10 percent of the teachers currently employed in the district, or 50 percent of the teachers in any one school. Their signatures do not imply that the teachers are willing to teach at the school or that they will be hired. The teachers' signatures are simply an indication that they support (or will not protest) the effort.

Next, you'll need to appear before the school board to win their approval. In the period from 1993 to 1998, founders who did not win the approval of their school board could not open a school; some districts made a practice of denying all petitions. The 1998 expansion of the charter school law allows groups to appeal this denial to their county office of education. Further appeals may be made to the state board of education. The legal body that grants the charter—district, county, or state board—is responsible for monitoring the school's performance, and withdrawing the charter if the school is not meeting the terms of its contract.

Advantages and disadvantages

2. *A new charter school is forming in our community. The parents of some of my children's friends are thinking of sending their youngsters. My two children are interested, but I'm nervous. Our district doesn't seem to allow choice, so my children attend neighborhood schools. They're not wonderful, but at least they're proven. What are the advantages of a charter school?*

All districts must provide choice (see chapter 9, "Choosing Schools"). If there is another school in the district that you want your child to attend, you need to put pressure on the district to advertise its open enrollment program—and, of course, apply to that school.

The enthusiasm for charter schools is fervent among believers. But the movement has opponents as well. Let's be fair and look at both the advantages and disadvantages of a charter school. First, the advantages:

+ Charter schools usually have a more consistent teaching philosophy than other schools. If you agree with the school's philosophy, that's an advantage. If you don't, don't even consider the school.
+ Accountability is built into the charter process. Charter schools must develop goals for student learning and performance standards, and they must evaluate the students' progress in meeting them. As a result, there is often a greater focus on learning and helping students to succeed. The parents' freedom to withdraw their children, and the district's (or whatever body approves the charter) power to revoke the school's contract, provide additional safeguards against nonperformance.
+ Parents usually play a stronger role in governance and in day-to-day operations.
+ Because they are usually smaller, charter schools are often better able to nurture a sense of community.

As to some of the disadvantages:

+ The enthusiasm of the founders may exceed their competence.
+ Charter schools often have problems attracting experienced teachers, who may be reluctant to risk job security and other protections. This is less of a problem in districts where teachers in charter schools are protected by the union contract.
+ Funding is a major concern for charter schools. Charter and regular schools receive the same state apportionment funding per student (an average of $5,584 per child), plus additional funds to support services for students in special education and other special programs for which the students or school qualifies. While this may allow the school to keep going, additional start-up funds are often needed. The 1998 legislation partially addresses this reality by requiring districts to make unused space available without charge to charter schools.

Interdistrict transfers

3. *There is a charter school forming in the next district that I'd like my child to attend. Do charters schools allow transfers across districts?*

Charters are not bound by district. They may accept students from any district within the state, with the exception that existing schools converted to charter status must give preference to students who live in the district. So the answer is, if this is a new school, you don't need to apply for an interdistrict transfer; just apply directly to the school. If it isn't a new school, you need to apply for a transfer.

Costs of attendance

4. How much will it cost me to send my child to a charter school?

Charter schools are public schools, which means they cannot charge tuition. However, you should be aware that charter schools face a host of operating expenses and start-up costs that can make them more expensive to run than regular district schools of comparable size. Rent often represents a significant expense. The 1998 revision requires districts to provide charter schools with free use of vacant facilities. Of course, when there aren't vacancies, space remains a problem.

Private school vs. charter schools

5. We are a group of 24 parents and 10 teachers who are interested in starting a K–8 school in the Central Valley. We're wondering if it's easier to succeed as a private school than to go through the charter school process?

Both are difficult. But if they're both possible, then I think the most fundamental distinction is financial. While established private schools have endowments, donors, and other sources of funding, new private schools are usually completely dependent on tuition and parent contributions. This can be a difficult hurdle to clear for any private school in its first few years. Charter schools, however, receive the same per-pupil funding as public schools—approximately $5,584 in 1998. So a major (if not total) portion of a charter school's budget is already covered.

Charter schools and private schools also differ in another fundamental way. Private schools are, frankly, more private. That is, they enable their boards to depart entirely from the community standards of the public whose taxes make charter schools possible. Charter schools, on the other hand, are accountable both to the board of the school it-self, and to the board that approved their charter. So if you are considering curriculum, methods of instruction, or employment practices that are far off the beaten path, you may be far happier creating a private school.

11 Freedom of Expression

In her elementary and middle school years, your child probably expressed herself just fine, without bumping into any school rules that might have confined her. However, at high-school age, students are feeling their collective oats. They have their own ideas, their own sense of style, and—one hopes—their own emerging sense of right and wrong.

As the parent of a teenager, you're living through the experience of your child at times defining herself in opposition to you. Each day may bring a new test: streaked hair, nose rings, tattoos, loud music, late-hour experiments in sleep deprivation. When these impulses of self-expression occur at home, you're the arbiter of good taste and the one who draws boundaries. But at school, it's teachers and principals who have that job. At some point in your teenager's life, you're likely to find yourself caught between your child and school authorities. This chapter is designed to help you cope with that moment of reckoning.

The issue may be religious expression. It may be a dress code. It may be that your tenth-grader's preferred book for an English assignment has been given the "thumbs-down" by her teacher. Or your son may have written an article for the school paper that won him a reprimand from the school principal. All these topics, and more, are considered to be issues of freedom of expression.

Fortunately, that freedom is, in principle, guaranteed by the Bill of Rights, the California Constitution, and various sections of the California Education Code. Yet securing these rights has never been without its difficulties. Concerned school administrators are constantly aware of the need to balance the rights of students against the need to keep order. Less concerned principals tend to quash individual expression first, and check with their district's lawyers later. Whichever type of principal you have, you'll be better prepared after reading the questions and answers that follow.

Perhaps this balancing act between students' rights and administrators' authority is best portrayed in the landmark 1969 case of *Tinker v. Des Moines*. During the early years of the Vietnam War, several high school students decided to wear black armbands as an expression of their dissent. Their principal learned of their plans in advance and adopted a policy that any student wearing an armband would be suspended. The students were indeed suspended and, in carrying their case to the Supreme Court, helped establish a core principle that would guide courts through many cases that would follow. The court ruled that students do not "shed their constitutional rights to freedom of speech or expression at the schoolhouse door." At the same time, the justices warned that students' rights to free speech were not absolute. This gave school officials fair grounds to weigh students' rights to free speech and expression against what the court termed a "comprehensive authority, consistent with fundamental constitutional safeguards, to prescribe and control conduct in the schools."

Because of the delicate nature of this balancing act, high school districts in California are required to set down very clear guidelines governing all aspects of student self-expression. Your district should make available to you and your child its policies on student publications, leafleting, demonstrations, dress code, body decorations, locker searches, and use of school buildings for student clubs and community meetings. Your child's school may also take the initiative to establish additional guidelines. Whatever they may be, you should find them to be consistent with the state and federal laws explained in the questions and answers that follow.

Questions and Answers

Banned books

1. *My daughter wanted to write a term paper on one of her favorite books,* One Hundred Years of Solitude. *The teacher refused because she said that the school board had banned the book from the curriculum, but it's still in the school library. What's going on?*

Court decisions related to banning books in the schools are very confusing. A teacher is allowed to deny a student the right to write a term paper on a book that the school board had banned from the curriculum.

The following grounds may be used to ban a book from the curriculum: it is inappropriate to the grade level, subject matter, and so forth; or offensive to the community's social, moral, or political values. However, books may not be banned simply because they are considered offensive to Christian ideology or promote some type of religious orthodoxy. The issue facing the courts is how to distinguish between the two: books that offend community values and those that are personally objectionable because of the ideas they contain. It is important to remember that books may only be banned by the school board, not by an individual teacher.

As to your finding the book in the library, Supreme Court decisions make it more difficult to remove books from libraries than from the curriculum. Because the school library is a resource for all courses and students of different ages, it has been more difficult to argue the inappropriateness of any particular book. Actually, based on how little money is available for school libraries—$3.95 per student in 1998— I'm amazed there are any books!

School paper censorship

2. *My son is one of the editors of the school paper. The last issue included an interview with some youths who are living on the street. The principal felt that "this is not the kind of information students should be exposed to" and demanded that the paper return to its previous format of reporting on dances, games, music, and school-sponsored activities. The editors claim "freedom of the press" and refuse to comply. What kind of trouble are they setting themselves up for?*

Trouble maybe, or perhaps meaningful preparation for careers in journalism or constitutional law. The California Education Code does not allow schools to censor a student publication—even one sponsored by the school—based on its content, unless the material might be considered obscene, libelous or slanderous, or publication of the material creates a clear and present danger of causing students to commit unlawful acts or to create a substantial disruption in the school (§48907). ("Obscene," "libelous or slanderous," and "substantial disruption" are all inexact terms whose definitions have been, and will continue to be, argued in the courts.)

The education code clearly limits the school's role. The journalism adviser is responsible for supervising the student staff to ensure that they maintain professional standards of English and journalism, and that the articles are not obscene, libelous, slanderous, or otherwise prohibited by law. The student editors are responsible for assigning and editing articles. Although the adviser may consider particular articles to be disrespectful, tasteless, offensive, or potentially damaging to the school's reputation, she cannot demand that articles be eliminated merely on these grounds.

Limits on distributing other publications

3. *When an underground newspaper published one of my son's articles, he brought about 40 copies of the paper to school to hand out in his English class. The teacher would not let him distribute these materials. Was she right?*

While she may not have been very sensitive to your son, and may have closed off a potentially interesting class discussion, her actions are justified under current interpretations of the law. Schools may only prevent students from distributing a publication if they can demonstrate that it contains material that might be considered obscene, libelous or slanderous, or likely to create a clear and present danger by causing

High School Paper Alleges Administrators' Abuse

A 1997 front-page story in the Palo Alto High School student newspaper, *The Campanile,* raised questions about administrators' credit card use. This prompted the superintendent of schools to ask the district's independent auditors to look into the allegations of malfeasance. The article and accompanying editorial alleged loose monitoring of credit card expenses and questionable charges. This was the second time in the past school year that *The Campanile* had targeted school district practices. Earlier, the newspaper had disclosed details of a closed school board meeting at which a $9,000 pay hike to a school district employee had been given. The raise was subsequently upheld in a public meeting.

While the district superintendent noted that he had no quarrel with young journalists probing district affairs, he felt that this latest article had an overtone of "personal statement not borne out by the facts," although the district did establish tighter controls on credit card use.

students to commit unlawful acts or to create a substantial disruption in the school.

As with any activity involving free speech, schools also have the right to adopt rules limiting the time and place where publications may be distributed. These are referred to as the "reasonable time, place, and manner" rules. Schools that are nervous about outside materials usually restrict distribution to before or after the school day, and out of the main traffic corridor.

It's really too bad the teacher could not recognize your son's accomplishment or share his enthusiasm.

Protest walkout

4. *My daughter and her friends organized a walkout to demonstrate their support for a favorite teacher who was being transferred to another school. When over 100 students gathered outside the building during school hours, the principal threatened to suspend all of them. Now their favorite counselor has been let go and the girls are planning another walkout. Do students have any rights?*

"Peaceable assembly" is a classic form of speech protected by the First Amendment. However, while students are allowed to demonstrate, schools may also limit the time, place, and manner of those demonstrations (§48950). The thousands of students who left school to demonstrate against the elimination of bilingual education risked disciplinary action for missing classes, but their speech, expressed mostly in public places off school grounds, was protected from censorship. Even demonstrations on school grounds are protected as long as what is said is not obscene, or libelous or slanderous, and as long as it does not create a clear and present danger of unlawful acts or substantial school disruption. While the students could be liable for having cut their classes, the punishment must conform to the usual penalty for missing one or more classes. Suspension seems unusually harsh.

Student groups' after-school meetings

5. *Other student groups meet at the school after hours, but when my son's prayer study group asked to use the building, the*

principal refused. I'm willing to chaperone all meetings. Why can't they use the building?

If other groups that are non-curriculum-related meet at school, so may prayer groups. In a court decision involving the San Diego Unified School District, the court ruled that student religious groups could use classroom space during non-instructional times to the extent to which other groups were permitted to meet. So, if other non-curriculum-related groups were permitted to meet in classrooms, your son's group is entitled to similar access. School districts may prevent religious groups from meeting at school only if they prohibit *all* non-curriculum-related groups from meeting there.

Ironically, your chaperoning complicates the issue. The federal Equal Access Act requires that student meetings be student-initiated, and that people from outside the school (like parents) neither lead, control, nor regularly attend the meetings. School staff members may attend these meetings so long as they act as observers and do not participate.

Parent-sponsored after-school activities

6. *Our school closes at 3:30, and even though our parents' group wants to sponsor after-school activities for the students, the principal refuses to let us use the building. She says that if she allows our programs to meet at the high school, anyone can come in. What can we do? We are willing to pay insurance and janitorial fees.*

Your request reflects some of the tension involved in applying the federal Equal Access Act to schools. (The Equal Access Act applies only to middle, junior high, and high schools, not to elementary schools.) In a 1989 decision, the Supreme Court ruled that once a school permits any non-curriculum-related student group to meet on its premises, it must extend this right to all other groups, and may not discriminate against particular groups—possibly including religious groups or even extremist organizations with which the school would not want to be identified. Your school is trying to avoid this issue by closing its doors to everyone.

One tactic you might use is to relate your activity to the school curriculum, since the Equal Access Act applies only to non-curriculum-related activities. You might want to talk with the principal about how your proposed activities relate to the school program. If you cannot find some relationship between your proposed activities and the curriculum and your principal refuses to allow non-curriculum-related activities to meet at the school, I suggest you find another place to meet.

Uniforms

7. *Most of the parents at our school want our children to wear uniforms. We think it will cut down on violence because the children won't be fighting over clothes, and it will certainly be cheaper for us. How do we institute a code without infringing on anyone's rights?*

Although the freedom to dress as one wants sounds like it should be protected by the Constitution, the courts have been reluctant to interfere with a school's authority to impose dress codes, particularly if the school justifies this measure in terms of reducing violence. This means that if your school decides to require uniforms, the decision must be based at least partly on the parents' and staff's sense that uniforms will reduce violence. Parents and students must be notified of the policy at least six months prior to its institution to give families time to prepare. The school must also let parents know that it will financially

---

Next Step—A Dress Code for Teachers

While Long Beach students were coming to school discreetly attired in blue-and-white uniforms, some of their teachers were dressed in torn clothes or beach attire. "For the most part, teachers dress appropriately," explained the executive director of the Teachers Association. Nonetheless, in May 1996, two years after adopting a policy requiring students to wear uniforms, the school board ordered schools to adopt guidelines for proper staff attire. Typical restrictions include no short shorts, tank tops, or other revealing attire, and no clothes that are torn or dirty. Some schools have adopted very detailed regulations; others merely stress that staff should appear neat, clean, and professional at all times.

assist families who cannot afford uniforms, and it must provide those parents who do not want their children to wear uniforms with a method of "opting out" of the program, that is, letting the school know that their child will not be following the dress code.

Public schools began requiring uniforms only in the mid-1990s, and we are just now gathering data that will allow us to evaluate the effectiveness of uniforms in reducing violence. In 1994, the Long Beach Unified School District became the first and largest public school district in the nation to require its elementary and middle school students to wear uniforms. District officials claimed that after instituting the dress policy, school crime plummeted by 76 percent; incidents of assaults plunged 85 percent; weapons offenses dropped 83 percent; and vandalism was cut by 50 percent.[56] The uniform policy also succeeded in increasing students' self-esteem, improving their behavior and attendance, and creating a better learning environment.

Punk fashion

8. *What about hairstyle, tattoos, nose rings? We've just moved into a new neighborhood—my children are well decorated, and I'm afraid that the school will refuse to admit them.*

If they are of school age, then the school must accept them. But I would venture that school officials could make life a little difficult for them and may ask that your children remove some of these articles. While personal appearance should be a personal decision, the courts don't like to interfere with a school's authority and usually uphold school rules in this area.

Gang crackdown or discrimination

9. *My son was stopped by a campus security guard for wearing a burgundy shirt, which the guard said was a "gang color." That's ridiculous. He's not in a gang. I think he was stopped not because of the color of his shirt but because of the color of his skin, because we're Latino. What rights do we have?*

Are you protesting the school's dress code or the discriminatory enforcement of that code? If it's the former, you'll have a hard time changing the policy. The California legislature has granted school districts the authority to adopt a "reasonable dress code policy that requires pupils to wear a schoolwide uniform or prohibits pupils from wearing gang-related apparel" (§35183). Individual schools and districts are responsible for defining "gang-related apparel" in their community.

If you don't believe in dress codes or codes prohibiting "gang colors," express your concerns to the school site council, if the code was developed at your local school. If you find that it's a districtwide policy, you'll need to address your concerns to your school board. And most importantly, you'll need to begin organizing.

Now, if it's a matter of discriminatory enforcement—only Latino students wearing burgundy are stopped—it's another matter. Before requesting a meeting with the principal and the school site council, you'll want to talk with other Latino students and their parents. You need an assurance from the school that the policy will be fairly enforced, and you—parents and students—must monitor their enforcement. If you are not satisfied with their answer or with the enforcement of the policy, you might want to seek legal assistance from one of the organizations listed in the legal services section of the parent resources appendix and organize other parents against this practice (see chapter 6, "Parent Involvement in School Governance"). Los Padres Unidos in Fresno tackled a similar problem; you may want to contact them for more information.[57]

Searches

10. *The other day, the campus security guard stopped my daughter and her friend and searched their book bags. After he was through and hadn't found anything, he said he thought they might be carrying stolen property. I told her she should have refused to open her pack. Was I right?*

Maybe. In general, the security guard's actions would be considered legal only if there were reasonable suspicion that the book bags contained a weapon, stolen property, or contraband (prohibited items). However, the American Civil Liberties Union (ACLU), which handles many such cases, warns students never to carry anything they don't want the police or school officials to know about.[58] They also advise students to make it clear that they refuse to be searched. While a student's refusal may not prevent the search, it may make the search illegal, which means that seized evidence may not be used in a criminal or juvenile proceeding (although illegally seized evidence may be used by the school in disciplinary proceedings). In other words, if your daughter did not consent to the search and the guard found stolen property, your daughter could be suspended (or expelled) but not charged in court.

How private are lockers?

11. *Yesterday, the assistant principal conducted a surprise search of the students' lockers and found some drugs in my son's jacket pocket. I know that young people should not use drugs, and they definitely should not bring them to school. My concern is the way they were discovered. Don't students have the right to keep things in their locker?*

School lockers are school property on loan to students by the school only lets students use them. Consequently, a search warrant or "probable cause" would not be needed to conduct a search. Your school should have distributed a written policy advising students and their parents that lockers may be searched from time to time for disciplinary, health, or safety reasons. The best advice is for students never to keep anything in a locker that they aren't willing to have discovered. Incidentally, some schools have dogs to search for drugs.

Drug tests for athletes

12. *Our school randomly tests athletes for drugs. When a urine test indicates the presence of drugs, the student is suspended from the team. I don't like drugs, but I'm uncomfortable with schools conducting urine tests. Is this legal?*

Yes, it is now. In 1995, the Supreme Court ruled that districts may perform random drug tests on student athletes without violating their constitutional rights. The Oregon school district that implemented this policy had argued that its purpose was to protect the health and safety of students and to provide drug users with assistance programs.

Dixon High School was the first California school to require that all students playing interscholastic sports—as well as cheerleaders—participate in random drug testing. Any student who fails the drug test must (a) bring his or her parent to a parent/student conference, (b) participate in an eight-week drug education program offered by an outside agency, and (c) not participate in the sports program for the rest of the semester. The penalties are doubled for the second violation.

Dixon's program has a strong mentoring component: athletes and cheerleaders from U.C. Davis lead workshops on drugs and sports for the student athletes. In turn, Dixon's athletes and cheerleaders serve as drug educators for athletes in the neighboring junior high schools. While the program has made huge inroads on the drug front, at least during the sports session, alcohol use has increased, according to Pete Sawyer, Dixon's coach.[59] (Urine tests cannot detect alcohol in the bloodstream.) "This is not only a school-wide problem, it is a community and societal problem. We try to change their behavior educationally, through role models, but it's not easy."

Although Dixon's program has been copied by other school districts, it should be noted that several federal suits are pending over schools that have conducted random drug searches.

Trouble
and Discipline

12 Suspensions, Expulsions, and Due Process

John, 15, had just completed his first week in high school when he was suspended for five days for slugging a boy who called his sister a name. John was a marginal student and could not afford to miss class. Because he was rushed out of school the day of the suspension, John did not have time to collect his books and assignments. The school would not let him make up his missed homework or tests, and he fell further behind. One month later, he was suspended again for failing to stop a fight. When John tried to explain that he was just an innocent bystander, the assistant principal reminded him of his record for fighting. The second suspension put John further behind in his schoolwork. By the time June rolled around, John had lost 20 days to suspensions and 10 days to illness. Not surprisingly, he failed three of his four classes. On his sixteenth birthday, he dropped out of school.

This chapter speaks to parents whose children are being disciplined—pulled from classes, held after school, suspended, or ultimately expelled—as well as those whose kids come home from school complaining that their school day is dominated by rowdies in the classroom and bullies in the hall. Both parents have real concerns, but very different ones.

In my talks with parents, I've heard many sad stories from well-meaning parents of kids in trouble. Their concerns center on two major issues. First, is their kid being given a fair shake? Is he really guilty of all that he's charged with? Has he been given a fair hearing? Does the punishment really fit the alleged crime? Second, these parents wonder whether the school is really trying to help their son, or whether they've decided he's just a bad apple who needs to be tossed from the barrel. This chapter is intended to help those parents make use of California education law and Department of Education rules to support their faith and see that their child is treated justly.

The chapter is also written for parents seeking some protection for their child who complains of rowdies run amok. Certainly, all kids are entitled to a school day free of havoc and disruption. Some situations require a parent to stand up for the rights of their children to have such a learning environment. Some of the questions and answers that follow should help you do just that.

Every school must develop a discipline code. This code should reflect state guidelines, school board policies, and the school community's approach to discipline. In developing this code, schools are instructed to "solicit the participation, views, and advice of one representative selected by each of the following groups: parents, teachers, school administrators, school security personnel, if any; and for junior high and high schools, pupils enrolled in the school." Final responsibility for approving the code has been given to the principal and a teacher representative (§35191.5). Both parents and students should receive a copy of the code at the beginning of each school year; a copy must also be filed at the district office. Schools are expected to review and approve their discipline code at least every four years.

Of course, there is a political dimension to all this as well. Legislators seeking easy routes to voter popularity occasionally posture as tough guys. One member of the California Assembly, after reading of the Singapore government's public caning policy, moved to adopt something similar for California schools. His objective: to bring back corporal punishment. Efforts to move his bill out of committee failed.

Some school officials have developed new approaches to discipline that work better than the older, harsher methods. These include in-school detentions, peer counseling, conflict mediation, and, at the high school level, student courts. But whatever disciplinary methods are employed, the goal is to teach students self-discipline rather than relying on outside controls.

This goal of student self-discipline is high on the list of what most schools aim for. Without it, learning cannot take place. Children cannot learn when students are insulting teachers or running uncontrolled through the halls. But on the other hand, effective schools are not places where teachers are constantly yelling at students, where students must always march in line, where large numbers of children are thrown out of school.

In effective schools, the staff has developed procedures for avoiding most discipline problems before they occur. The cornerstone of good discipline is a reasonable discipline code policy that clearly states the kinds of behavior that will not be permitted. The code must be distributed and repeatedly explained to teachers, students, and parents, so that it will be apparent to everyone when a student's behavior is out of line and what the consequences are for breaking the rules.

But a good discipline code is only the first step. A written code, even a very good one, means nothing unless it is carried out consistently. The same behavior by different children, at different times, in the presence of different teachers, must be treated the same way. Parents know, of course, that absolute consistency is impossible, and that on a good day you can laugh at something that drives you crazy on a bad day. But if students believe that the way discipline is administered is arbitrary—that certain teachers have it in for them or that certain kids can get away with anything—the school will have constant discipline problems.

A good discipline code should be specific to the school, yet consistent with the rules and procedures developed by the district and state. To do this, the legislature suggests that the school solicit the "participation, views, and advice" of parents, teachers, school administrators, school security personnel, and (if the school is a middle or high school) students in developing the policy (§35191.5[a]).

In response to court cases, and student and parent concerns, the federal and state government have developed guidelines that schools must follow before a student can be suspended. Students and their parents have the right:

- ⬥ to be given notice of the charges;
- ⬥ to respond to the charges; and
- ⬥ to attend a pre-suspension conference at which the school summarizes the evidence against the student and the student has an opportunity to explain his side of the story, with the exception that a student may be immediately suspended when the school believes that he presents a danger to other people or property, or threatens to disrupt the class. The suspension conference must then be scheduled as soon as possible.[60]

The guidelines regulating expulsion are more extensive, and are outlined in the answer to question 7.

Questions and Answers

Grounds for suspensions

1. *Our school has had a discipline code on our books for years, which we automatically renew every few years. While it has some good rules, it really doesn't reflect today's reality. We are trying to develop a new code. Is there anything that must be included? Expulsion cases are handled by the district, so we're only looking at suspension.*

The legislature has given the schools the authority to suspend students for a long list of offenses:

+ damaging or stealing school property;
+ possessing or using alcohol;
+ committing obscene acts or habitually using profanity;
+ possessing or selling drugs or drug paraphernalia;
+ disrupting school activities or willfully defying school authority;
+ stealing, attempting to steal, or knowingly receiving stolen property;
+ possessing an imitation or real firearm or weapon;
+ sexual harassment;
+ hate-motivated behavior; and
+ gang activities

The district may include additional offenses. A student may be suspended for any of the above offenses if they occur on school grounds;

Zero Tolerance?

The following offenses merited a suspension under the zero-tolerance policy. Do you agree that these are the kinds of serious offenses that merit a suspension?

The first-grader who kissed his classmate—suspended for sexual harassment.

The 10-year-old student who carried a kitchen knife to school to slice her chicken for lunch—suspended for carrying a weapon.

The high school student who gave her friend a Midol (an over-the-counter drug for reducing menstrual cramps)—suspended for distributing drugs.

The 11-year-old who wrote essays in his English class about killing the principal and burning the school—suspended for five days for terrorist threats.

while going to or coming from school; during lunch period, whether on or off campus; and during or on the way to or from a school-sponsored activity (§48900).

The key word in that last sentence is "may." The decision to use suspensions and when to suspend students is highly discretionary. Some schools and districts view suspension as a last resort, only to be used when other means of reforming the student's behavior have not worked. A first-time offender may be gently reminded that "we don't act that way in school." Parent-teacher conferences, a visit to the principal's office, and other approaches may be tried before the school considers it necessary to suspend the child.

Some schools and districts practice "zero tolerance": a student who commits any suspendable offense is automatically suspended, whether the child is a first-time offender or a chronic troublemaker.

Due process rights

2. *My son complains that when students get caught doing something wrong, they never get a chance to tell their side of the story. What is supposed to happen before a student may be suspended?*

A school's discipline code should address both the causes for suspension and the procedures that must be followed before a suspension can take place, including a notice of the charges against them and an opportunity to respond to the allegations. The school must make an effort to notify the parent before their child is suspended so that the parent may attend the pre-suspension conference (unless, as mentioned earlier, the child presents a danger to himself or property, in which case the conference may take place after the child has begun serving the suspension).

Some schools ask that parents accompany their child to classes when they return after a suspension. While parent involvement is certainly a worthwhile goal, a student whose parent cannot take the time off must still be allowed to return to school.

Schools are allowed to suspend a student for a total of 20 days per school year. Suspensions are limited to five consecutive school days per offense, except (a) when the parent agrees with the school that the student presents a danger or threat of disruption, or (b) when the student is being transferred to a continuation school. The principal and the school disciplinarian (usually the assistant principal) are the only staff who can order a student suspended.

Class suspensions

3. *There is one English teacher in our school who always sends my daughter to the principal's office. The assistant principal has been very sympathetic and usually finds some work for Maria. While I appreciate what he's doing, I'm sure my daughter could benefit from attending English class—if not this class, then another. What can I do?*

You and Maria need to come to an understanding with her teacher. If it appears that they will never be able to work together, request that the school transfer Maria to another class. It sounds as though the assistant principal would be willing to help.

Suspensions by a teacher from her class are not restricted to the 20-day limit imposed on suspensions from school. However, like other suspensions, they require a suspension conference with the student and parent. These conferences may occur after the suspension has taken place.

Suspension for emotional disability

4. *Five months ago, the school and I agreed that my daughter should be placed in a classroom for emotionally disturbed youngsters. Unfortunately, the special education class is overcrowded, so her placement has not been changed. When Tami gets tense, she begins walking around the classroom. Every time this happens, she's suspended. What can I do?*

This is one of the most hotly debated issues in special education. By suspending your daughter for behavior related to her handicap, your school is seriously out of compliance with federal and state guidelines on special education. A 1988 Supreme Court decision (*Honig v. Doe*) ruled that exclusion of a disabled student from school for more than ten days represents a change of placement and thus requires the procedural safeguards available under special education legislation. That means that your daughter must remain in her classroom until you and the school have agreed to a new IEP, unless the district can prove a substantial likelihood that her actions will hurt herself or others.

Ask for an immediate meeting with the principal and insist that an appropriate placement be found. If the school cannot honor your request, consult one of the special education assistance groups listed in the appendix on parent resources.

I would assume that your daughter's teacher is not the only teacher who has problems relating to special education students. You might want to ask the school site council to address this issue in the annual site plan, by specifying that classroom teachers receive training to help them work more effectively with special education students mainstreamed into their classes. Be sure to insist that these suspensions be removed from your daughter's record—and remember to check her file to make sure they are. (See chapter 8, "Access to Information: Records.")

Suspensions in emergency situations

5. *My son was suspended for four days for throwing a pencil to his friend across the room. The suspension conference was scheduled for the day before the end of his suspension. When I protested, the principal explained that this was an "emergency situation" and that Mike threatened the other child's life. That's a bit extreme. His friend needed a pencil and my son threw him one. What is an emergency situation?*

An emergency situation is anything that, in the school's estimation, "constitutes a clear and present danger to the life, safety, or health of pupils or school personnel." From your description, it definitely doesn't sound like the pencil-throwing episode met that definition.

For now, you should insist that the principal erase the suspension from your son's record. If something like this should happen again, demand that the school schedule an earlier conference and immediately reinstate your son. Make sure you invite any other student who was involved to the meeting so that all parties can explain what really happened.

If the school does not agree to reinstate your son, you and/or your child may appeal. A suspension may be challenged on the following grounds:

- the school did not follow the due process procedures (summarized in the answer to question 1 above);
- the student was suspended for violating a rule he did not know existed;
- the school policy does not specify suspension as the penalty for the behavior in question;
- school rules are arbitrarily enforced, or there appears to be a pattern of racial discrimination; or
- the student is handicapped and the behavior for which he was suspended relates to that handicap (see answer to previous question).

Then schedule an immediate meeting with the district superintendent to appeal the suspension and the procedures (or lack thereof) followed by the school. If you are not satisfied with the superintendent's response, you may want to call one of the legal services listed in the appendix on parent resources.

Chronic suspensions

6. *Last year my 10-year-old son was suspended for a total of 15 days for minor offenses like chewing gum or talking back to teachers. That's a lot of time to be out of school. The pattern has begun again this year. I'm concerned, because I don't want him home alone. I'm also concerned that he's falling behind in his schoolwork. What can I do?*

To understand the source of the problem, talk with your son and his teachers. Are there things you, your son, or his teachers could do to make school something he looks forward to each day? Are events outside of school upsetting him and causing him to "act out"? If the problem cannot be resolved at this level, discuss your concerns with the principal and the school site council (see chapter 6, "Parent Involvement in School Governance"). As the only school body with governing authority, the council is an appropriate group to participate in developing and reviewing your school's discipline policies.

Let the school know that you are aware of your right to attend a pre-suspension conference. Also inform them that if your son is suspended, you want him to bring his homework with him so that he can complete any assignments, and to have an opportunity to make up tests missed during the suspension. Insist that his grades not be lowered if he adequately completes his assignments and passes the exams. Lowering grades represents a double punishment and has been challenged by a number of parent organizations. You might also check his school records to make sure that these suspensions are described accurately and fairly. (See chapter 8, "Access to Information: Records.")

Because sending a child home often means sending him into an unsupervised situation or penalizing parents by making them stay home, many schools are implementing other alternatives, such as an in-school suspension room (during or after school hours), community service in lieu of suspension, or Saturday class. The new regulation eliminating excused absences—including those related to suspension— should motivate all schools to develop in-school suspension programs. (See chapter 7, "Who Gets Schooled.") Remember, no matter how grateful you might be that your child is still in school, the due process rights described above also protect students assigned to in-school programs.

In addition to talking with other parents to learn how discipline is handled at their schools, your school district should maintain school-by-school statistics on suspensions. You need to review that report. If another school has a lower suspension rate, try to talk with some of its parents and visit the school. They may be doing something that could be helpful in your school, or their low suspension rate might indicate a school where no one maintains discipline, or anything in between. And, of course, they may not be accurately reporting what's going on. The *Good Common School Book*, published by the National Coalition of Advocates for Students, offers a number of suggestions to help parents organizing around school discipline.[61]

New expulsion policy and procedures

7. *My son has been repeatedly suspended, and now his principal is threatening to expel him. What are our rights?*

First, a principal may not expel a student; he can only recommend expulsion. The decision to expel can only be made by the school board. Second, recent legislation has drastically altered the definition of expulsion.

Until recently, an expulsion effectively removed a student from school. In 1995, however, the legislature passed a resolution forcing school districts to provide an alternative placement for expelled students. This act became effective in July 1996.[62] Because an expelled student must be allowed to continue his education, though not at his present school, districts have opened community schools and other alternative programs at off-campus sites.

The student's school or district is also required to develop an individual rehabilitation plan for the student before expelling him. The plan must address the requirements the student must meet before being allowed back into the regular program (e.g., daily attendance, completing all homework, attending a drug treatment program, and so on). The plan may also specify that the family attends counseling and parenting classes.

You and your son may certainly challenge the expulsion. As with any legal challenge, a student facing an expulsion has the right to: (a) be notified of the charges against him; (b) be represented by counsel; (c) review and obtain copies of all documents prior to the hearing; (d) present and question witnesses and evidence; and (e) receive a transcript of the hearing.

Expulsion cases are heard in closed session by a committee of the school board or by an impartial hearing officer. The hearing must take place within 30 school days after the student has been charged, unless the family requests more time to prepare their case. The committee or hearing officer's recommendation is submitted to the board, which has 10 school days to decide whether to expel the student or to suspend the expulsion order. The student's family then has 30 school days to appeal a negative decision to the county board of education. The student may attend school during this time, with the superintendent's consent.

California has identified three kinds of actions for which a student *must* be expelled: carrying a firearm, threatening another student or staff member with a knife, or selling drugs. Under proposed legislation, school board members who *do not* expel a student found committing any of these offenses could be subject to a $1,000 fine, a six-month jail term, or both. In addition to the above three offenses, school boards have the authority to develop their own list of offenses for which students will be expelled. A copy of the list should be distributed to all students, parents, and teachers.

Expulsion is a serious matter. I suggest you look for an attorney or an advocate to advise and assist you in this situation.

Assignment to dangerous school

8. *After my 15-year-old son was expelled, we were informed that he must attend a school across the city. His life will be in danger if he goes there. What are our choices?*

Present your concerns to the school board and ask them to place him in a program in a safer area. If the district cannot find a suitable program, request that they transfer him to a program in a neighboring district. While districts once suggested independent study for expelled students, home study is no longer considered an alternative to expulsion, since many students who were assigned to it never opened their books.

School districts are increasingly concerned about their legal responsibility to provide an education, so the board should be willing to help the two of you find another program.

School choice after expulsion

9. *When my son was expelled last year, the district placed him in a special program with academic support and counseling. Now we're told that he has to return to his regular school. If he goes back, I think he'll just get into trouble again. Do we have any other alternatives?*

Yes, you do. After the term of expulsion, and if the school board determines that your son does not present a danger to other students or the staff, he has the same right to choose a school as enjoyed by any other student. (See chapter 9, "Choosing Schools.")

Classroom anarchy

10. *My daughter's high school seems to have given up on disciplining students. Classrooms are chaotic. Teachers just seem to ignore students who are talking and acting out. What can we do?*

If a school has a clear plan for discipline that is actually carried out, teachers are more likely to take major responsibility for making the plan work day-to-day. They know that they aren't on their own—that they will be backed up if they discipline children for not following the rules. They will feel confident in disciplining a student anywhere in the school, instead of walking past problems.

Teacher passivity when students are out of control—in class and in the halls—is one reason parents, school boards, and school staff have gone to the extreme of insisting on zero tolerance of any infraction. By ignoring bad behavior, teachers demonstrate and perpetuate the low expectations they hold for their students.

You need to get involved with the school discipline committee. If no such committee exists, go to the school site council (see chapter 6, "Parent Involvement in School Governance"). It will take the work of concerned parents to effect this change. I'm sure some teachers are as frustrated as you are and will support your effort.

Dangerous classroom

11. *We just enrolled our eleven-year-old in a middle school that doesn't seem to believe in suspensions. Her classroom is so dangerous she's afraid to attend.*

That's obviously not right. You need to spend some time observing the class so that you have a clear sense of what's really happening —whether your daughter is overwhelmed by the newness of the experience or the class really is out of control. If it's the latter, then you will want to transfer her to a more orderly classroom. If you cannot find a better situation in her school, you may want to apply for a transfer to another school (see chapter 9, "Choosing Schools").

Whatever you decide to do, it's important that you express your concerns to the principal and the school site council. They need to be aware of the problems students are facing in the school.

Striking a child

12. *One student in my son's class really seems to annoy the teacher. The other day, she hit him. Is a teacher allowed to strike a child?*

No, corporal punishment is prohibited in California schools. The child's parent should immediately report this behavior to the superintendent and the school board so that it can take appropriate action.[63] (See chapter 5, "Educators and Their 'Customers'.")

Withholding grades

13. *My daughter destroyed about $2,000 of lab equipment when her chemistry experiment exploded. She claims it was an accident. The school insists that it was deliberate, and says we must cover the costs or they will not release her grades. Can they do that?*

Yes, they can. School districts may withhold grades, transcripts, and your daughter's diploma if they can prove that it was really deliberate, and if you refuse or are unable to pay for the damages. Furthermore, any school in the state that your daughter transfers to must also enforce this penalty. Schools are encouraged to provide a program of voluntary work if the family cannot make the payment. Before any of this can occur, however, the school needs to prove its charge at a due process hearing (§48904). I suggest you hire an attorney to bring to that hearing.

Praise

14. *I think our school handles discipline really well, or at least I don't have any complaints. I'm called in when there's a problem. My son gets to tell his side of the story. Basically, they follow the rules. But it would be nice to hear when he does something well. How do other schools handle that?*

It's really important that schools praise students for behaving well, for helping out, for helping each other. Some principals insist that teachers call parents when their child has done something special. Other teachers haven't waited for a directive from the school. They know that parents appreciate being told when their child is doing well. A phone call, a note home, e-mail—all help to create a more positive environment for learning.

13 Safety and Order

Five-year-old Johnny Smith was excited about starting kindergarten at Bridges Elementary, his neighborhood school. The Smiths had visited the school and decided that Mrs. T would be a good teacher for Johnny. Several of the neighboring children had spoken of having very positive experiences in her class. Johnny had also visited the school, inspecting the books and toys in the classroom.

Then in May, their seven-year-old neighbor complained to his mother that some fifth-graders had threatened to beat him up after school. Although the child's mother had complained to the principal, the principal had not intervened, and the threats continued. The little boy refused to go to school unless his mother walked with him in the morning and waited for him in the afternoon.

Despite their high regard for Mrs. T's teaching ability and their interest in having Johnny attend the neighborhood school, the Smiths, like thousands of parents throughout the United States, decided to investigate other alternatives.

Ask parents whether their child goes to a good school and most often the answer you'll hear is either "Yes, it's a safe school" or "No, it's dangerous. I wish he didn't have to go there." "Safety is paramount for most parents," explains one educator. "I can understand it, but I wish they looked at the learning, too."

The intense concerns of parents, staff, and students about school safety have sent school administrators and politicians scrambling to respond. As long ago as 1982, California voters added the following provision to the California Constitution: "Right to Safe Schools. All students and staff of primary, elementary, junior high and senior high schools have the inalienable right to attend campuses which are safe, secure and peaceful."[64]

Since then, nearly every district has done something to make schools safer and more conducive to learning, but only some of these efforts have proven effective. To find out whether a school has successfully created a safe climate, talk to the people at the school as well as out in the neighborhood.

I suggest you first talk with the students—whether third-graders or twelfth-graders, they'll all have a point of view. Every school allows parents on school grounds to observe or volunteer. (Remember to stop at the school office to let them know you're at the school. Some schools ask visitors to call for an appointment before coming to school.) Observe the halls and playground. Ask the students if they like being in school and if it's a safe place to be. Kids, like adults, will compare the school scene with the scene outside school. That, in fact, is the most telling benchmark for comparison. You'll be hard pressed to find a school where every child feels perfectly safe, of course. But it's fair to expect that the school community has succeeded in creating a place where it feels safer inside the walls than outside. Ask the teachers how they feel, what they've observed, and about any incidents that may have happened on campus.

Principals *must report* anything resembling a crime to the district for compilation in the annual California School Safety Report, issued every February and available from the California Department of Education. Review statistics for all the schools in the community. Most principals have subscribed to one violence prevention program or another. You may want to see the program in action or attend one of the training sessions. You will certainly want to ask what its impact has been: What area of violence is the program intended to address? And how well has it succeeded?

Many schools work hard at providing an "island of safety" in an otherwise dangerous neighborhood. For students who walk, bike, or take public transportation to school, or who leave school during lunch, the safety of the neighborhood matters immensely. If you are concerned, spend time in the neighborhood. You may even want to visit the local police department to review their crime statistics or simply to discuss your concerns with a police officer.

Before going on to the questions and answers, I'd like to affirm one factor that seems to be present at every truly safe school: the school responds to any threat to its security with confidence and as a whole community. This is not hollow rhetoric. "Confidence" is tangible and recognizable. It is the absence of fear. Students and staff walk with eyes forward. They have no need to look over their shoulders, either figuratively or literally. Students and staff show the same sense of lightness that is present when people are secure and in comfortable surroundings.

A school that is "responding as a whole" is a bit harder to describe, but it lies in the absence of conflict between teachers and principals, between parents and staff, and between students and staff. A school community is not unlike a large boat. In a safe school, all the members of the school community have learned how to row together.

Questions and Answers

<u>Safety to, from, and after school</u>

1. *We live in a dangerous neighborhood, and I am afraid every day when my ten-year-old leaves for school and when she walks home. I work all day, so I can't go with her, but I insist that she call me as soon as she gets home, and that she remain inside all afternoon. I realize the school can't be responsible for everything that happens on the street, but this is a horrible fear to live with. Can anything be done?*

I assume there is no school or public transportation that your daughter might use, or if there is, it's not any safer; and that you've already looked into asking her to walk with friends. Schools in similar neighborhoods have asked the police department to assign extra officers to patrol the routes to and from school during the morning and afternoon hours. In one southern California community plagued by drive-by shootings, morning and afternoon parent patrols join the police in monitoring street corners.

Schools and nonprofit community agencies also offer on-site after-school programs (e.g., child care, tutoring, mentoring, team sports, gymnastics, arts and crafts) so that parents are not forced to choose between insisting their children remain home after school and worrying about them being out on the streets.

KID SMARTS and QUICK CALLS, two programs developed by St.

John's Educational Thresholds Center (SJETC), help protect community youth in one of San Francisco's most dangerous neighborhoods.[65] KID SMARTS, organized several years ago in response to a series of attacks on elementary and middle school students attending the Center's after-school program, offers classes in safety and survival skills. The local police department, and other city and community agencies conduct monthly workshops on street safety and self-defense, kidnap prevention, safe and responsible bus riding, home safety, fire safety, and emergency medical services.

QUICK CALLS is a friendly-neighbor program in an area where small businesses must compete with street crime. Stores that are willing to make an emergency call to a student's parent, the police, or for an ambulance indicate their participation by displaying a hot pink QUICK CALLS sign in their window. The sign is credited with averting at least one disaster. When a youngster was assaulted on the street by two adults, his sister ran to a store displaying the QUICK CALLS sign. The owner's quick call to the police saved the student from more severe injuries.

You may want to work with other parents, a community agency, and the school to design similar programs in your neighborhood. (See the appendix on parent resources.)

Schoolyard bullies

2. *For the past month, a group of older children has been harassing the first-graders during recess. First there was teasing and shoving, then books were snatched. Later some children were forced to hand over their milk money. Two teachers are assigned to recess duty, but we have a large playground with hidden corners, and I guess they can't see everything. Any solutions?*

Schools have a legal duty to provide a safe environment for their students. This includes supervising youngsters during recess. While parents have successfully sued schools whose supervision was insufficient or inadequate, you need a more immediate response. Perhaps you and other parents can volunteer in the playground. If this is not possible, encourage your child to stay within eyesight of a teacher or other adult.

Ask the principal how he plans to address the problem. He may be willing to assign extra teachers to the schoolyard, schedule separate recess periods, restrict a section of the playground to younger students, and so on. Longer-term solutions—"buddy" programs, mixed-age groupings where students of different ages participate together in special activities—provide opportunities for positive interaction between older and younger students. Conflict resolution programs and peer counseling have also proved successful in some schools. Work with the principal and school site council to create a program that meets your school's needs.

Parents also need to teach their children how to take care of themselves in dangerous situations. The school can help by sponsoring parenting workshops and parent support groups. A community agency may be eager to assist with this effort.

Conflict resolution

3. *My son came home the other day very proud that he had been appointed a "conflict manager" and that he was responsible for making sure that there are no fights at recess. While I agree that it's wonderful, he's still only nine years old. Shouldn't the teachers be doing this instead of turning it over to the children? Could Tom get hurt?*

No, I don't think Tom will get hurt. Conflict managers at the elementary school are usually well supervised by the staff. The goal of a conflict management program is to train students to talk through their conflicts, rather than relying on their fists. The managers remind students to use these skills, and, at times, even help them talk through their problems. Conflict management or resolution programs are most effective when students respect one another, and they are respected by their teachers. Nine-year-old conflict managers cannot create a healthy and safe school climate. At best, they can support it.

Some schools incorporate conflict management in the curriculum. Some even offer parent workshops so that these skills can be reinforced —and even practiced—at home. The Community Board Program of San Francisco has developed an extensive curriculum that may be used with teachers, students, and parents in grades K–12.[66]

I think both you and Tom can be proud of his willingness to assume this responsibility. If the school hasn't already introduced parents to the program, you might suggest that one be scheduled. And remember, you can visit the school to see the program in action.

Student courts

4. *I remember hearing about student courts and how they cut down on violence. What are they?*

Student courts, sometimes called youth courts, are courts staffed by young people. They act as the jury, the bailiff, attorneys, and sometimes the judge. These courts are also recognized by the state as a "diversion program" and have the full authority of a court of law.

The Placer County Peer Court program has both a courtroom and a school component, with the latter integrated into the high school curriculum as a credit-bearing course. (School districts that offer a teen or peer court program in cooperation with the court, probation department, district attorney, and public defender may use this program to fulfill part of the requirements for a unit on the American legal system [§51220.2].) A two-week unit introduces all high school freshmen to the courts, the legal system, and the peer court. Cases are argued by student attorneys and decided by student juries—with input from consulting attorneys. Students' sentences range from sitting on a minimum of two peer court juries (this use of jury service as a punishment says a lot about the general perception of our jury system) to a one-year suspension of the student's driver's license. At times, the court even sentences parents to attend parenting classes and to pay for drug testing.

Placer County's peer court has been recognized as an exemplary program by the United States Congress, and its curriculum has been approved by the California Department of Education and the state legislature.[67]

Guns in the schools

5. *My daughter says that students have brought guns to her high school. Short of installing a metal detector, what can be done?*

As long as weapons are readily available, they pose a threat in the schools. Metal detectors are, as you probably know, expensive to install and operate and, to be effective, would have to be placed at every entrance to the campus. ID cards, a closed campus, improved in-school communication, and police patrolling the halls are just some of the strategies schools have used to protect students and staff.

San Francisco's Washington High School, the largest high school in the city, attributes reduced violence and an improved school environment to its 24-hour hotline. Developed in response to students' complaints about the threats they received when they left campus for lunch, and the intimidation they feared if they reported these incidents, the hotline gives students a fear-free reporting mechanism. The hotline (a voice mailbox answered by the assistant principal and costing only $20 per month) gives students an opportunity to express their concerns from the privacy of their homes, a pay phone, or wherever they feel safe. Students call in reports of violence, threats, vandalism, and other problems. The hotline is also used by parents and neighbors, concerned by things they have overheard or observed. Callers in need of more intensive help are referred to other resources (for example, counselor was notified when a student contemplating suicide called the hotline). Washington High School staff members credit the hotline with helping solve two murders; thwarting drug deals, suicide attempts, and extortion; and alerting staff to students carrying weapons.[68]

Restroom drug sales

6. *My son tells me that drug deals take place in the second-floor boys' restroom during lunch. I realize that he might be exaggerating, but should I call my friend in the police department?*

Ask the principal to check it out first. Boys' restrooms are a recognized problem area and should be supervised. Many principals are reluctant to involve the police in school affairs because they feel that it unnecessarily involves children in the law enforcement system, and reflects negatively on their school's reputation and their own reputation as a competent manager. If no action is taken and the problem continues, make that call.

Threat or free speech

7. *My daughter threatened to "punch out" her counselor when the latter refused to fill out a tardy slip that would have allowed her*

back into class. Not only did the counselor report her to the principal, but she also filed a police report. Now my daughter's in real trouble. What can we do?

I'd suggest calling an attorney. Under state law, the counselor had no choice but to report your daughter's threat: a staff person who does not report an incident of violence or threatened violence faces a $200 fine. While it may still be possible for you and your daughter to work something out with the school administration, your daughter's understandable, though inappropriate behavior may expose her to some disciplinary action.

A San Diego high school student, after a frustrating afternoon going from one administrative office to another to have her schedule changed, threatened to shoot her guidance counselor when the latter informed her that the change would not be allowed. When the counselor reported the incident, the school responded by suspending the student. In turn, the girl's parents filed a lawsuit asserting that their daughter's First Amendment right to free speech had been violated.

The trial court decision was appealed to the U.S. District Court of Appeals, which initially ruled in the girl's favor, awarding damages and erasing the suspension. Three months later, however, the court reversed itself, finding that the student's statements "directly and unambiguously threatened physical harm." I don't know what this tells you about the wisdom of turning to the courts, but I hope it reinforces the seriousness of the charge.

<u>Teaching tolerance</u>

8. *Our middle school has really changed over the last five years, from an almost all-white student body to over one-third Vietnamese and Mexican. There have been a lot of racial slurs, even some fighting. What can we do?*

Racism and intolerance are not easy topics to discuss. Often, it helps to bring in outside people trained in these matters to initiate and direct the discussion in a positive, constructive manner. I'm familiar with the STAR program (Students Talk About Race), a project of People for the American Way.[69] STAR recruits and trains college volunteers to lead discussions on racism and sexism in high school and middle school classrooms.

Ask the school to consider providing multicultural training for the teachers, other staff, students, and parents. Your county office of education or the California Department of Education may be able to suggest some consultants. Don't forget to ask outside community organizations for their support. You will probably find that they have also been trying to address the problem. Informal efforts organized by parent groups—such as organized potlucks, international dinners, and buddy programs—can also contribute to improved communication within the parent and student communities.

But whatever you come up with, there are two essential ingredients in defusing an explosive tension among the student body. First, the principal must have a strong commitment to peace between student factions. Second, staff must unite to make that commitment come to life—translating strong words into even stronger actions.

The forces that lead students to be uptight toward fellow students from other backgrounds are powerful. Expecting those tensions to dissipate in the face of words alone is simply unrealistic.

Harassment of gay students

9. *My son wants to drop out of school because other students are taunting him about being gay. When I told him to report the problem to the principal, he said that would only make it worse. He's scared and hurt. How can I protect him?*

You need to get the school to take action—for your son and for other youths who may be in a similar situation. Unfortunately, although many schools have instituted appropriate policies, few have established the necessary procedures to back them up. One exception is the San Francisco Unified School District. Under the direction of a full-time staff person, Services for Sexual Minority Youth provides an anonymous phone line, a resource directory, books, and other teaching materials that focus on family diversity, the promotion of an "anti-slur" policy, incorporation of issues around sexual and family diversity in the curriculum, a teacher training program, and the designation of a staff member on every campus who can listen to students and provide emotional and practical support.[70]

Harassment by classmates

10. *For the past month, my fifth-grader has complained that the boys in her class have been teasing her about her looks. The counselor advised her to ignore them. She feels miserable. Can't the school make the boys stop?*

They should certainly try. Harassment—whether perpetrated by adults or kids—is, unfortunately, an all too common problem. A parent of an elementary school student in Antioch won a lawsuit against the school district for the sexual harassment of his daughter by a classmate. Three years earlier, a male sixth-grade classmate had begun tormenting her with obscene gestures, name-calling, and violent threats.

"I saw the fear in her eyes," her father said. "I had to do something." After a fruitless attempt to persuade school officials to counsel the boy and stop the harassment, the family hired an attorney and ultimately was awarded $500,000 in damages.

Many districts have also started to take peer harassment (what we used to call "taunting") more seriously in recent years. So far, however, only a handful of peer-harassment lawsuits have reached a jury and, unlike the Antioch case, the damage awards have been fairly small. Schools have responded by passing directives prohibiting peer harassment, and some are seeking guidance on how to prevent peer sexual and other harassment.

For further information, you can contact the National Training Associates in Sebastopol, a consulting firm assisting schools in addressing these issues.[71] The NTA training program is available for students, school staff, and parents.

Sexual molestation by teacher

11. *Last night my 13-year-old told me that one of the teachers at her school sexually molested her. My first response would be to drag the man out of class and kill him. Other suggestions?*

Take a deep breath and walk through the following steps, even though they are emotionally less satisfying. Report the offense to the police so that they can start a criminal investigation. They may also refer you to Child Protective Services (CPS). Notify the principal. Let him know that you will take action if he doesn't take immediate and appropriate action against the teacher. The principal should suspend the teacher pending the outcome of the court investigation. A teacher who is convicted of molesting a student goes to prison, and will lose his teaching credential. If he is not convicted, he will receive the back pay he lost while the case was under investigation. Teachers who molest students have been successfully prosecuted, and school districts have been sued for not taking immediate and appropriate action.

In a 1996 decision involving a fourth-grade teacher accused of molesting nine students, the Berkeley Unified School District agreed to revise its policies and procedures regarding staff response to complaints of sexual harassment and abuse of students, and to train school district administrators, teachers, and other certified personnel regarding such harassment and abuse. The school district also paid at least $1.15 million to the plaintiffs in this case.

Because districts are hesitant to accuse teachers of offenses that have not been proven in court, molesters used to be afforded a relatively safe passage through the school system. In the past, teachers who were accused of molesting students were encouraged to transfer to another district. Recently, however, the California Supreme Court unanimously ruled that school districts that have knowledge of charges of molestation and do not inform the teacher's future employers may be sued.

Students stealing from students

12. *My 10-year-old brought one of her birthday presents to school the other day, and somehow it "disappeared" from her locker. This is the third time this year that she's "lost" something from her locker. She suspects that it was taken by the student she shares her locker with. How can I help her be more careful?*

I'd first suggest that the two of you agree that valuables are too tempting to be brought to school. Since she suspects that her locker partner might have taken the items, she should ask the teacher to change her assignment. (She may need your support in making this request.) After she is reassigned to a locker of her own, buy her a new lock and have her practice opening and closing it before bringing it to school. Students sometimes get careless or are in a rush and just hang the lock in place, without actually closing it. With a little practice, she may find it easy enough to actually use it.

Notes

1. For example, a staff person with the Sacramento City Unified School District's Parent Community Partnership Center schedules math and science nights to introduce the curriculum to parents. The Center's phone number is (916) 433-5275; fax (916) 433-5276.

2. Q.E.D.—Research-Based Advocacy for Academic Excellence is one parent organization that has serious concerns about the "new" and "new new" math; you can reach them by telephone at (805) 969-6139 or by e-mail at Greens@west.com.

3. Parent Educational Resource Center, (650) 655-2410; fax: (650) 655-2411.

4. California Community Foundation, 606 S. Olive Street, Los Angeles, CA 90014; (213) 413-4042, or fax: (213) 383-2046, as reported in *Education Week*, December 3, 1997.

5. Children's Book Project, 45 Holly Park Circle, San Francisco, CA 94110, Tel. (415) 647-2042.

6. CPEE, P.O. Box 19744, Sacramento, CA 95819-0744, Tel. (916) 454-0212, Web: http://members.aol.com/CPEECAL, or e-mail: CPEESAC@aol.com.

7. In addition to increased graduation requirements, Challenge school districts must also agree to develop and adopt content and performance standards at every grade level; adopt clear accountability measures; build partnerships with parents, businesses, and communities; and move critical decisions to the school and district level. In return, districts may obtain waivers from those provisions of the education code or federal regulations that hamper their efforts. For further information, contact the Challenge Initiative Coordinator at (800) 700-5850.

8. California Education Code §51215(10)(g): "Standards of proficiency shall be adopted by the governing board with the active involvement of parents [who are] broadly reflective of the socioeconomic composition of the district, administrators, teachers, counselors, and, with respect to standards in secondary schools, pupils."

9. "Unfinished Business," The Achievement Council, 3460 Wilshire Boulevard, Suite 420, Los Angeles, CA 90010, Tel. (213) 487-3194.

10. California Arts Council, 1300 "I" Street, Suite 930, Sacramento, CA 95814, Tel. (916) 322-6555.

11. State Committee of Practitioners for Title I, Diane Raulston, 8015 Greenly Drive, Oakland, CA 94605, Tel. (510) 569-6778.

12. Accelerated Schools, CERAS 109, Stanford University, Stanford, CA 94305-3084, Tel. (650) 725-1676; hf. cys@forsythe. stanford.edu.

13. For additional information, contact Oakland Health & Bioscience Academy, Oakland Technical High School, 4351 Broadway, Oakland, CA 94611; (510) 879-2663 or (510) 879-3059; fax: (510) 879-3059.

14. Complaints Management Services, California Department of Education, P.O. Box 944272, Sacramento, CA 94244-2720, Tel. (916) 657-2754; Office for Civil Rights, 50 United Nations Plaza, Room 239, San Francisco, CA 94102, Tel. (415) 437-7700.

15. CAPS, a project of the Center for Law and Education, 1875 Connecticut Avenue, N.W., Suite 510, Washington, DC 20009, Tel. (212) 986-3000, Fax (202) 986-6648.

16. Equal Rights Advocates, Tel. (415) 621-0505 or their hotline (800) 839-4372.

17. California Interscholastic Federation — State Office: 664 Las Gallinas Avenue, San Rafael, CA 94903, Tel. (415) 492-5911; Southern California Office: 425 East 18th Street, #9, Costa Mesa, CA 92629, Tel. (714) 574-0924.

18. United States Department of Education, Office for Civil Rights, 50 United Nations Plaza, Room 239, San Francisco, CA 94102, Tel. (415) 437-7700.

19. "Whenever any part of the instruction in health, family life education, and sex education conflicts with the religious training and beliefs of the parent or guardian of any pupil, the pupil, on written request of the parent or guardian, shall be excused from the part of the training which conflicts with such religious training and beliefs. As used in this section, 'religious training and beliefs' includes personal moral convictions" (California Education Code §51240).

20. California Education Code §51201.5. "The governing board of each school district . . . shall provide the parent or guardian of each pupil in grades 7 to 12 . . . with written notice explaining the purpose of the AIDS prevention instruction. The notice shall specify that any parent or guardian may request that his or her child or ward not receive instruction in AIDS prevention. No pupil shall be required to attend the AIDS prevention instruction if a written request that he or she not attend has been received by the school."

21. Education Code §54422.

22. META, Inc. (Multicultural Education, Training and Advocacy Inc.), letter to Senator Greene and members of Senate Education Committee, 6/24/96.

23. You can get information on the GED exam by calling (916) 327-0037.

24. In 1995, 10.4 percent of students eligible for special education services (ages birth–22 years) and 9.34 percent of the state's 6- to 21-year-olds were enrolled in special education. Over two-thirds of California's special education students attend regular classes for at least half the day.

25. California Education Code §51216(d): "Instruction in basic skills shall be provided for any pupil who does not demonstrate sufficient progress toward mastery of basic skills and shall continue until the pupil has been given numerous opportunities to achieve mastery."

26. California Department of Education, December *Special Education Enrollment Data,* August 1, 1996.

27. A class preparing teachers for mainstreaming is required for teachers to earn a "professional clear" or regular teaching credential. (See chapter 5 "Educators and Their 'Customers'.")

28. California Commission on Teacher Credentialing, P.O. Box 944270, Sacramento, CA 94244-2700, Tel. (916) 445-7254.

29. Commission on Teacher Credentialing, *Waiver Handbook,* Feb. 1996.

30. "Putting Qualified Teachers In Every Classroom," Richard M. Ingersoll, *Education Week,* June 11, 1997.

31. Community Partners for Educational Excellence, CPEE Update, April 1995. CPEE may be contacted at P.O. Box 19744, Sacramento, CA 95819-0744, Tel. (916) 454-0212, e-mail: CPEESAC@aol.com; also see their Web site at http://members.aol.com/CPEECAL.

32. A. Henderson and N. Berla, "A New Generation of Evidence: The Family Is Critical to Student Achievement" (National Committee for Citizens in Education, 1994). NCEE publications are now distributed by the Center for Law and Education in Washington; refer to the appendix on resources for contact information.

33. Programs that require an SSC as a condition for receiving and expending supplemental funds are the School Improvement Program (SIP; California Education Code §52000–52049); School-Based Coordinated Program (SBCP; §52800–52888); and Motivation and Maintenance Program (SB 65 —Dropout Prevention; §54720–54734).

34. For information and assistance in establishing parent involvement programs and family-school compacts at the school or district level, contact the Family and Community Partnerships Office, Tel. (916) 657-3768.

35. Complaints Management Services, California Department of Education, P.O. Box 944272, Sacramento, CA 94244-2720, Tel. (916) 657-2754.

36. VICCI Program, Lowell High School, Tel. (415) 759-2730.

37. California Education Code §48011: "A child who . . . has been admitted to

the kindergarten maintained by a private or a public school in California or any other state, and who has completed one school year therein, shall be admitted to the first grade of an elementary school unless the parent or guardian of the child and the school district agree that the child may continue in kindergarten for not more than an additional school year . . . if the child is at least five years of age."

38. HomeSchool Association of California, P.O. Box 2442, Atascadero, CA 93423, Tel. hotline (805) 462-0726, voice mail (707) 765-5375, e-mail: hscinfo@aol.com; Web: http://members.aol.com/hsconline.

39. California Education Code §49067(b): "The governing board of any school district may adopt regulations authorizing a teacher to assign a failing grade to any pupil whose unexcused absences from the teacher's class equal or exceed a maximum number which shall be specified by the board."

40. California Education Code §48900(m)(4): "It is the intent of the Legislature that alternatives to suspensions or expulsion be imposed against any pupil who is truant, tardy, or otherwise absent from school activities."

41. California Association of Student Councils, 1212 Preservation Park Way, Oakland, CA 94612; phone: (510) 834-2272; fax: (510) 834-2275; www.xm.com/casc/.

42. California Education Code §48260.5: "Upon a pupil's initial classification as a truant, the school district shall notify the pupil's parent or guardian, by first-class mail or other reasonable means, of the following: (a) That the pupil is truant. (b) That the parent or guardian is obligated to compel the attendance of the pupil at school. (c) That parents or guardians who fail to meet this obligation may be guilty of an infraction and subject to prosecution. . . . (d) That alternative educational programs are available in the district. (e) That the parent or guardian has the right to meet with appropriate school personnel to discuss solutions to the pupil's truancy. (f) That the pupil may be subject to prosecution. (g) That the pupil may be subject to suspension, restriction or delay of the pupil's driving privilege. (h) That it is recommended that the parent or guardian accompany the pupil to school and attend classes with the pupil for one day."

43. SARBs are operated by school districts, although a probation officer may sit on the SARB panel.

44. Los Angeles Unified School District, Fact Sheet, June 6, 1996.

45. Rohnert Park has developed a packet of information on their daytime curfew program, which they are willing to share with interested schools, cities, and parents. Contact the Rohnert City Department of Public Safety, Youth and Family Services, 500 City Hall Drive, Rohnert Park, CA 94928-2118; (707) 584-2699.

46. A recent study by the Justice Policy Institute in Monrovia painted a different picture. "Police reports released as part of a lawsuit filed by Monrovia parents showed that youth crime actually jumped by 53 percent during the school year that the curfew was in force, and dropped 12 percent in summer months when the curfew was suspended. Dan Macallair, who authored the report, said one reason for this may be that free youth recreation programs are provided during the sumer. These programs are more comprehensive than those found in many other California cities—positive intervention rather than what he calls the "negative approach of a curfew."

47. For more information, contact the Department of Education, (916) 657-2451.

48. The California Education Code (§52901[a]) in fact encourages school districts that offer alternative programs for school dropouts to "utilize the resources and expertise of community-based organizations that deal with youth and young adults."

49. California Proficiency Testing is a private company contracted by the California Department of Education; you can reach them at (916) 383-9506.

50. California Education Code §48800.5(a) and (b): "A parent or guardian of any pupil, regardless of the pupil's age or class level, may petition the governing board of the school district in which the pupil is enrolled to authorize the attendance of the pupil at a community college as a special full-time student on the ground that the pupil would benefit from advanced scholastic or vocational work that would be available. If the governing board denies the petition, the pupil's parent or guardian may file an appeal with the county board of education, which shall render a final decision on the petition. . . . A parent or guardian of a pupil who is not enrolled in a public school may directly petition the president of any community college to authorize the attendance of the pupil at the community college as a special part-time or full-time student on the ground that the pupil would benefit from advanced scholastic or vocational work that would thereby be available."

51. Contact the Family Policy Compliance Office, U.S. Department of Education, 600 Independence Avenue, SW, Washington, DC 20202-4605.

52. *Education Week,* (Special Report) "Charter Schools," November 29, 1995.

53. The 1998 legislation opens the door to 125 additional schools over the next year, plus 100 additional charter schools each school year after that.

54. Charter Schools —Works in Progress, EdSource Report, April 1996.

55. EdFact Executive Summary, EdSource, April 1996.

56. *Education Week,* January 21, 1998.

57. Los Padres Unidos, 2054 East El Palo Avenue, Fresno, CA 93720, Tel. (209) 297-4219.

58. The American Civil Liberties Union–Northern California chapter distributes a free publication for students on their rights, "We Have Rights Too! But What Are They?" Contact ACLU-NC, 1663 Mission Street, Suite 460, San Francisco, CA 94103, Tel. (415) 621-2493; Complaint Desk: (415) 621-2488.

59. Pete Sawyer, Dixon High School, Tel. (916) 678-2391.

60. California Education Code §48911(b): "Suspension by the principal . . . shall be preceded by an informal conference conducted by the principal or the principal's designee . . . between the pupil and, whenever practicable, the teacher, supervisor, or school employee who referred the pupil to the principal. At the conference, the pupil shall be informed of the reason for the disciplinary action and the evidence against him or her and shall be given the opportunity to present his or her version or evidence in his or her defense."

61. The Good Common School Project, National Coalition of Advocates for Students (NCAS), 100 Boylston Street, Suite 737, Boston, MA 02116, Tel. (617) 357-8507, fax (617) 357-9549.

62. California Education Code §48916.1: "At the time an expulsion of a pupil is ordered, the governing board of the school district shall ensure that an educational program is provided to the pupil for the period of the expulsion"; and §48916(b): "The governing board shall recommend a plan of rehabilitation for the pupil at the time of the expulsion order, which may include, but not be limited to, periodic review as well as assessment at the time of review for readmission. The plan may also include recommendations for improved academic performance, tutoring, special education assessments, job training, counseling, employment, community service, or other rehabilitative programs."

63. California Education Code §49001(b): "No person employed by or engaged in a public school shall inflict, or cause to be inflicted corporal punishment upon a pupil."

64. California Constitution, art. 1, §28(c).

65. St. John's Educational Thresholds Center, 3040 - 16th Street, San Francisco, CA 94103, Tel. (415) 864-5205.

66. Community Board Program, 1540 Market Street, Suite 490, San Francisco, CA 94102, Tel. (415) 552-1250.

67. For information on the Placer County program, contact Peer Court Office, 671 Newcastle Road, Suite 7, Newcastle, CA 95658, Tel. (916) 663-9227.

68. For more information about this program, contact Washington High School; (415) 750-8400.

69. STAR (Students Talk About Race), People for the American Way, 2000 M Street N.W., Suite 400, Washington, DC 20036, Tel. (202) 467-4999 or, in California, (310) 823-2860; e-mail: pfaw@pfaw.org; Web site: http://www.pfaw.org.

70. For more information, contact the School Health Programs Department, San Francisco Unified School District, 1512 Golden Gate Avenue, San Francisco, CA 94115, Tel. (415) 749-3400.

71. National Training Associates in Sebastopol can be reached toll-free at (800) 624-1120.

Appendix 1

Resources
A Directory of Organizations

Parent and Student Resources

Parent and Student Groups, California-Based

The following organizations are representative of the variety of ways in which parents are involving themselves in their children's education. They have been arranged alphabetically for ease of reference, and should by no means be considered an exhaustive listing. Find out from other parents the names of groups in your community—or consider forming a parent group of your own! And let us know, so that we may add you to our database, and refer interested callers to you.

Area Congregations Together (ACT)
Jim Keddy (916) 488-1138
Ron Snyder (510) 639-1444
A grassroots organization of parents, community members, and religious leaders focusing on educational issues of concern to low-income communities. Each group defines its own issues. Projects in Anaheim, Contra Costa County, Costa Mesa, Fullerton, Oakland, Riverside, Sacramento, San Bernardino County, San Diego, San Francisco, San Jose, San Mateo County, Santa Ana, and Stockton. Call Keddy or Snyder for a phone number of a parent group working in your area.

California Association of Student Councils
1212 Preservation Park Way
Oakland, CA 94612
tel. (510) 834-2272
fax (510) 834-2275
e-mail: cascmail@aol.com
Web: http://www.xm.com/casc/
Statewide high school leadership organization, representing almost all California high schools.

Center for Parent Involvement in Education (CPIE)
Parents Union
Walter Kudumu
4749 Federal Boulevard, Suite F
San Diego, CA 92102
tel. (619) 264-8828
fax (619) 264-8825
e-mail: cpie@pacbell.net
Committed to improving the academic achievement of African-American children. Key programs: advocacy training for parents, leadership training, neighborhood education watch, and other activities to increase parent involvement in education.

Community Alliance for a Responsible Educational System (CARES)
372 Hull Avenue
San Jose, CA 95125
Andrea Villasenor-Perry (408) 995-5302
Linda Ramsden (408) 287-2827
Working with parent and community groups on issues of accountability, academic achievement, and greater parent involvement in governance and decision-making. San Jose Unified School District.

Community Partners for Educational Excellence (CPEE)
P.O. Box 19744
Sacramento, CA 95819-9744
Beverly Lamb (916) 454-0212
Maureen Fitzgerald (916) 392-8083
e-mail: CPEESAC@aol.com
Web: http://members.aol.com/CPEECAL
Educational policy-making at the district and state level; committed to building a well-informed and effective parent voice. Key issues: funding levels, school calendar, site-based decision-making, state standards, and accountability. Sacramento City Unified School District.

Equal Voice for Parents
Terry Gibson
921 Elsinore Drive
Palo Alto, CA 94303
(650) 493-2170

Promoting parents as partners in the education of their children. Key issues: curriculum, textbook selection, and finance. Palo Alto Unified School District.

HomeSchool Association of California
P.O. Box 2442
Atascadero, CA 93423
hotline (805) 462-0726
voice mail (707) 765-5375
e-mail: hscinfo@aol.com
Web: http://www.hsc.org
Supports and promotes home schooling, providing information, monitoring legislation, and helping families new to home-schooling start their own schools. Produces publications and sponsors an annual conference.

Los Padres Unidos
Margie Robles
2054 East El Paso Avenue
Fresno, CA 93720
(209) 297-4219
Sponsors workshops for Hispanic youth: Boys-to-Men Conference, Hispanic Student Women's Conference, teacher workshops. Clovis Unified School District.

Parents Advocates for Children's Education (PACE)
Gary Redmann
417 Mace Boulevard, Suite J-250
Davis, CA 95616
(530) 756-9058
Provides forum to prepare parents to assume a more active role in school affairs; developed a mentor project to assist newly active parents. Key issues: curriculum and assessment. Davis Joint Unified School District.

Parents for Unity (PFU)
Marcy Sanz
P.O. Box 19151
Los Angeles, CA 90019
tel. (323) 734-9353
fax (323) 735-8105

Liaison between school, local, state, and federal governments; assists local parent groups; provides leadership training and assistance with grievance resolution. Los Angeles Unified School District.

Parent-Teacher Association (PTA)
P.O. Box 15015
Los Angeles, CA 90015
tel. (213) 620-1100
fax (213) 620-1411
e-mail: ptacala@aol.com
Web: www.capta.org
Oldest parent organization, the PTA provides a forum for parents, teachers, and school administrators to work together. Information on schools, current education issues, and parenting. PTA chapters exist in most schools, and chapter membership is open to all people with an interest in educational issues, including high school students. The PTA is a nonprofit organization funded by annual membership dues and local fundraising events.

Woodland Community Partners for Education (WCPE)
Brad Gollober
926 Fairview Drive
Woodland, CA 95695
(916) 668-6135
Trains parents to sit on school district committees; researches issues coming before school district board. Key issues: parent involvement in decision-making, instructional time, finance, collective bargaining, principal and teacher accountability, youth violence/conflict resolution. Woodland Joint Unified School District.

Curriculum-Related Organizations

Accelerated Schools
CERAS 109
Stanford University
Stanford, CA 94305-3084
tel. (650) 725-1676
e-mail: hy.cys@forsythe.stanford.edu
Web: http://www.stanford.edu/group/ASP

Publishes newsletter, provides technical assistance to schools to help them develop an accelerated program for at-risk students. Favors an approach that moves faster and more intensively with students who are lagging, in contrast to traditional "go-slow" remediation.

California Arts Council
1300 "I" Street, Suite 930
Sacramento, CA 95814
tel. (916) 322-6555
fax (916) 322-6575
Web: http://www.cac.ca.gov
A state agency funding artist-in-residence programs.

California Association for the Gifted
426 Escuela Avenue, Suite 19
Mountain View, CA 94940
tel. (650) 965-0653
fax (650) 965-0654
e-mail: admin@gifted.org
Web: http://www.cagifted.org
Statewide organization of parents and educators committed to appropriate educational opportunities for gifted and talented students. Services include publications, teacher training and certification, research grants, student scholarships, and advocacy at all levels of government.

California Interscholastic Federation
Web: http://www.cifstate.org
State Office:
664 Gallinas Avenue
San Rafael, CA 94903
(415) 492-5911
Southern California Office:
425 East 18th Street, #9
Costa Mesa, CA 92629
(714) 574-0924
Coordinates and monitors interscholastic sports and setting of standards for participation.

Community Board Program
1540 Market Street, Room 490
San Francisco, CA 94102
(415) 552-1250
e-mail: cmbrds@conflictnet.org
Web: http://www.igc.org/igc/conflictnet/index.html
Provides schools and youth-serving agencies, in California and throughout the country, with the staffing and materials to implement and maintain conflict resolution programs, curricula, and peer mediation programs.

Mathematically Correct
P.O. Box 22083
San Diego, CA 92192-2083
Web: http://ourworld.compuserve.com/homepages/mathman
Provides a wealth of information to help parents challenge the "new new math."

People for the American Way
2000 "M" Street, N.W., Suite 400
Washington, DC 20036
(202) 467-4999
in California, (310) 823-2860
e-mail: pfaw@pfaw.org
Web: http://www.pfaw.org
STAR (Students Talk About Racism) is a project of People for the American Way. STAR recruits college volunteers to lead discussions on racism and sexism in high school and middle school classrooms.

Disability Rights Groups

DREDF (Disability Rights Education and Defense Fund)
2212 Sixth Street
Berkeley, CA 94710
phone: (510) 644-2555
e-mail: dredf@dredf.org
Web: http://www.dredf.org
Serves the East Bay area, providing legal representation, training, information and referrals, and advocacy.

Exceptional Parents Unlimited
4120 North First Street
Fresno, CA 93726
(209) 229-2000
e-mail: epu1@cybergate.com
Serves the Central Valley area.

Matrix: A Parent Network and Resource Center
555 Northgate Drive, Suite A
San Rafael, CA 94903
(415) 499-3877
e-mail: matrix@marin.k12.ca.us
Web: http://www.marin.org/html/education.html

Parents' Educational Resource Center (PERC)
1660 South Amphlett Boulevard, Suite 200
San Mateo, CA 94402-2508
tel. (650) 655-2410
fax (650) 655-2411
e-mail: perc@netcom.com
Web: http://www.perc-schwabfdn.org
Provides information and guidance to parents and others seeking resources to help students with learning differences gain self-esteem and maximize their potential in school and other life activities.

Parent Training and Information Centers:
Parents Helping Parents (San Francisco)
594 Monterey Boulevard
San Francisco, CA 94127
(415) 841-8820
Parents Helping Parents (Santa Clara)
3041 Olcott
Santa Clara, CA 95054
(408) 727-5775

Team of Advocates for Special Kids (TASK)
100 West Cerritos Avenue
Anaheim, CA 92085
(714) 533-8275
Serves the area from Bakersfield to the Mexican border.

State Organizations Providing Advocacy, Research, Information, and Other Assistance

The Achievement Council
3640 Wilshire Boulevard, Suite 420
Los Angeles, CA 90010
tel. (213) 487-3194
fax (213) 487-0879
e-mail: kathcross@aol.com
Web: http://www.achievementcouncil.com
Works with individual schools and districts to help educators and parents close the achievement gap between students in urban schools and their suburban counterparts; advocates for students in the community, with educational policymakers, and in the schools. Focuses on southern California.

California Tomorrow
Fort Mason Center, Building B
San Francisco, CA 94123
tel. (415) 441-7631
fax (415) 441-7635
Web: http://www.californiatomorrow.org
In-depth research, advocacy, and technical assistance to build a society that values racial, cultural, and linguistic diversity. Publications on immigrant students, school restructuring, youth services, and early childhood education, with local examples of model programs to help parents and schools take the next step.

Children Now
1212 Broadway
Oakland, CA 94612
tel. (510) 763-2444
fax (310) 268-1994 (note different area code)
e-mail: children@dnai.com
Web: http://www.childrennow.org
A nonpartisan, independent voice for California children. Publishes report card on the well-being of California children; works with media to improve news coverage about children. Useful information, though education per se is not on the group's agenda.

Coleman Advocates for Children & Youth
2601 Mission Street, #804
San Francisco, CA 94110
tel. (415) 641-4362
fax (415) 641-1708
e-mail: coleman@sirius.com
Web: http://www.thecity.sfsu.edu/~coleman
Organization that spearheaded passage of San Francisco's Children's Amendment, guaranteeing a percentage of the city's budget for children's services; provides funding for advocacy on local children's issues as well as information on starting local child advocacy organizations and initiatives.

Ed-Data Education Partnership
Web: http://www.ed-data.k12.ca.us
Offers the latest fiscal, demographic, and performance data about California's K–12 public schools. Excellent source for facts about school districts and schools.

EdSource
4151 Middlefield Road, Suite 100
Palo Alto, CA 94025
(650) 323-8396
e-mail: EdSource@aol.com
Web: http://www.edsource.org
Publishes a monthly fact sheet on education issues, and annual "Resource Cards" with updated data. Major focus on school finance. Sponsors annual conference. Materials are concise and useful, and strive to be impartial.

PACE (Policy Analysis for California Education)
School of Education
3653 Tolman Hall
University of California
Berkeley, CA 94720
tel. (510) 642-7223
fax (510) 642-9148
e-mail: PACE123@violet.berkeley.edu
Web: http://www-gse.berkeley.edu/research/PACE/pace.html
Independent, nonpartisan, university-based (Stanford and U.C. Berkeley) education policy research center. Extensive publication list.

State Committee of Practitioners for Title I
Peggy Rodriguez
California Association of Compensatory Education
(916) 653-1327
Web: http://www.cde.ca.gov => see "community"
Assists parents in developing school and district Title I advisory committees; provides workshops and training for parents on their rights and responsibilities under Title I.

State of California Department of Education
560 "J" Street
Sacramento, CA 94244
Web: http://www.cde.ca.gov
Frequently used numbers:

Information:	(916) 657-2451
Public Information:	(916) 657-3027
Superintendent:	(916) 657-4766
Elementary Schools:	(916) 657-3351
Middle Schools:	(916) 657-4399
High Schools:	(916) 657-2532
Charter Schools:	(916) 657-5142
School Safety:	(916) 323-1117
Special Education:	(916) 445-4602
Choice:	(916) 657-2757
At-Risk Youth:	(916) 323-2212
Legal Office:	(916) 657-2453
Family and Community Partnerships:	(916) 657-3768
Healthy Start:	(916) 657-3558
Complaints Management Services:	(916) 657-2754
Title I (District and School Support):	(916) 657-2577

School Wise Press
236 Moncada Way
San Francisco, CA 94127
tel. (415) 337-7971; (800) 247-8843
fax (415) 337-1146
e-mail: info@schoolwisepress.com
Web: http://www.schoolwisepress.com

A wealth of information to help parents get smart about California schools. Offers rankings of all public schools within all California counties, guides to the school choice laws, pointers to other sources of information, local newspaper articles, and more.

National Public Interest Organizations Providing Advocacy, Research, Information, and Other Assistance

Center for Education Reform
1001 Connecticut Ave, N.W., Suite #204
Washington, DC 20036
tel. (202) 822-9000 or (800) 521-2118
fax (202) 822-5077
Web: http://www.edreform.com
Advocates for vouchers, charters, and expanded school choice. Their executive director, Jeanne Allen, is the author of their parent guide, "The School Reform Handbook."

Center for Law and Education
1875 Connecticut Avenue, N.W., Suite 510
Washington, DC 20009
tel. (202) 986-3000
fax (202) 986-6648
e-mail: cledc@erols.com
Web: http://www.cleweb.org
Materials for attorneys and lay persons on education law, policy, and practice; monitors federal legislation. Priority areas: Title I, academic reform, school-to-work/vocational reform, education of children with disabilities, tracking, testing, and parent/student/community involvement. CLE has assumed the distribution of materials formerly published by the National Committee for Citizens in Education (NCCE).

Community Action for Public Schools (CAPS), a new project of the Center, helps to link parents, educators, students, advocates, and others committed to the right to high-quality education. Publishes a newsletter on school reform, information on legal rights, and legislative alerts; links callers with the names of groups working on similar issues or involved in their area.

Center on School, Family, and Community Partnerships

Johns Hopkins University
3505 North Charles Street
Baltimore, MD 21218
tel. (410) 516-8800
fax (410) 516-8890
e-mail: nnps@csos.jhu.edu
Web: http://www.csos.jhu.edu/p2000
Publishes studies for parents and educators on school issues and partnership-related concerns. Also provides training and technical assistance to help schools develop more effective partnerships with families and the community.

Children's Defense Fund

25 "E" Street, N.W.
Washington, DC 20001
tel. (202) 628-8787
fax (202) 628-8333
Web: http://www.childrensdefense.org
The nation's leading child advocacy organization. Publishes reports, newsletters, and action alerts; holds annual conference. Useful, well-written materials, though education per se is not on the group's agenda.

FAIRTEST: The National Center for Fair and Open Testing

342 Broadway
Cambridge, MA 02139
tel. (617) 864-4810
fax (617) 497-2224
e-mail: FairTest@aol.com
Web: http://www.fairtest.org
A nonprofit public education and advocacy organization working to eliminate flaws in, and misuses of standardized multiple-choice tests.

Institute for Educational Leadership (IEL)

1001 Connecticut Avenue, N.W., Suite 310
Washington, DC 20036
tel. (202) 822-8405
fax (202) 872-4050
e-mail: iel@iel.org

Web: http://www.iel.org
IEL brings together educators, civic leaders, business executives, parents, and public officials in partnerships on behalf of children and youth. Sponsors a number of projects, all of which produce publications.

Institute for Responsive Education
Northeastern University
15 Nightingale Hall
Boston, MA 02115
tel. (617) 373-2595
fax; (617) 373-8924
Web: http://www.resp-ed.org
National research and development organization that promotes parent, community, and family involvement in school reform. Publications list and information packets available.

National Coalition of Advocates for Students (NCAS)
100 Boylston Street, Suite 737
Boston, MA 02116
tel. (617) 357-8507
fax (617) 357-9549
Web: http://www.ncas1.org
A coalition of advocacy groups committed to achieving equal access to a quality public education for vulnerable students, particularly those who are poor, children of color, recently immigrated, or differently abled. Publishes books, newsletters, and other materials, and sponsors several national projects.

Parents for Public Schools
P.O. Box 12807
Jackson, MS 39236-2807
tel. (800) 880-1222
fax (601) 982-0002
e-mail: PPSChapter@aol.com
Web: http://www.pps.net
A national organization of grassroots chapters dedicated to supporting, strengthening, and promoting public schools in communities throughout the United States. Local chapters focus on recruiting families to enroll their children in the public schools, and are committed to increasing productive parent involvement in decision-making for school improvement districtwide.

Public Agenda
6 East 39th Street
New York, NY 10016-0112
tel. (212) 686-6610
fax (212) 889-3461
e-mail: paresearch@aol.com
Web: http://www.publicagenda.org
Conducts studies and produces public opinion polls specifically on educa-
tion. Best known for highly valuable comparative studies of the views of
teachers, parents, school board members, and the public.

Legal Referral Agencies and Selected Legal Services

On those occasions when you are unable to resolve your problems or
differences with the school or school district, you may want to consult
an attorney. To find one, contact your local county bar association
and request someone with experience in education law or civil rights
(or whatever area best fits your complaint). Attorneys on the referral
list may see you for an initial visit at a nominal charge to discuss your
problem. Often one meeting can give you enough information to let
you know how to proceed. In addition to the county bar association
lawyer referral services, almost every county has a Legal Services Office
providing free legal services in civil matters to low-income families,
including assistance on problems relating to schools, discrimination,
and civil rights. Consult your local phone book for the number of
your county's Legal Services Office. If you cannot find a listing, call
the State Bar Public Relations Department at (415) 561-8399, ext.
7418, or your county's bar association lawyer referral service for an
appropriate referral.

The following are just some of the legal services resources that
may be available:

Alliance for Children's Rights
3333 Wilshire Boulevard, Suite 420
Los Angeles, CA 90010
(213) 368-6010
Must be low-income.

American Civil Liberties Union of Northern California (ACLU-NC)
1663 Mission Street, Suite 460
San Francisco, CA 94103
(415) 621-2493
Complaint Desk: (415) 621-2488
Web: http://www.aclu.org => "states"
Strongest national advocates of civil liberties, First Amendment rights, and issues of social justice.

American Civil Liberties Union of Southern California
1616 Beverly Boulevard
Los Angeles, CA 90026
(213) 977-9500
Web: www.aclu.org => "states"
Strongest national advocates of civil liberties, First Amendment rights, and issues of social justice.

California Rural Legal Assistance (CRLA)
Central Office:
631 Howard Street, Suite 300
San Francisco, CA 94105
(415) 777-2752
e-mail: hn0097@handsnet.org
Web: http://www.crla.org
Sixteen field offices statewide. Must be low-income.

East Palo Alto Community Law Project
1395 Bay Road
East Palo Alto, CA 94303
(650) 853-1600
Serves youth in East Palo Alto and East Menlo Park. Must be low-income.

Equal Rights Advocates
1663 Mission Street, Suite 460
San Francisco, CA 94103
tel. (415) 621-0505; (800) 839-4ERA
fax (415) 621-6744
e-mail: eraadvocates@earthlink.net
Web: http://www.equalrights.org

Advocates of equal rights for women, specializing in civil rights and economic rights.

Legal Services for Children (San Francisco)
1254 Market Street, Third Floor
San Francisco, CA 94102
(415) 863-3762
Must be low-income.

Legal Services of Northern California
515 - 12th Street
Sacramento, CA 95814
(916) 443-3391
Must be low-income.

Serving Specific Constituencies:

California Indian Legal Services
510 - 16th Street, Suite 301
Oakland, CA 94612
(510) 835-0284
email: cilsoakland@telis.org
Serves Indian youth and parents in Northern California.

Centro Legal de la Raza
Educational Empowerment Program/Latino Student Rights
1900 Fruitvale Avenue, Suite 3-A
Oakland, CA 94601
(510) 261-3721
Serves the Latino community.

MALDEF (Mexican American Legal Defense and Education Fund)
National Headquarters:
634 S. Spring Street, 11th Floor
Los Angeles, CA 90014
(213) 629-2512
Web: http://www.latinoweb.com/maldef
Serves the Latino community nationally and locally, specializing in advocacy and law. Known for their strengths: serving lawyers who are, in turn, taking cases where issues of social justice are at stake.

San Francisco Office:
182 Second Street, Second Floor
San Francisco, CA 94105
(415) 543-5598

Computer Resources

Computer Recycling
1275 Fourth Street
Lock Box 200
Santa Rosa, CA 95404
(408) 327-1800
North Bay Area nonprofit that accepts gifts of computer hardware and finds them a home. Only nonprofits and schools are qualified recipients. Focus is Marin, Sonoma, and Napa counties.

CompuMentor
89 Stillman
San Francisco, CA 94107
(415) 863-8827
Web: http://www.compumentor.org
Specialists for ten years in finding and matching volunteer computer consultants with schools and nonprofits that need their assistance. Also donates software to members for cost of handling and shipping.

Community Computing Cooperatives
1465 Donner
San Francisco, CA 94124
(415) 822-4144
email: ccciowii@pacbell.net
In San Francisco will donate refurbished computers to local churches, nonprofits, and schools.

Computer Recycling Center
589 Mendocino Avenue
Santa Rosa, CA 95401
tel. (707) 575-8273
fax (707) 575-5955
Receives any and all computer equipment, working or not. Sells computer equipment to the public schools or nonprofits.

Marin Computer Resource Center
757 Lincoln Avenue, Units 18 & 19
San Rafael, CA 94901
tel. (415) 454-4227
fax (415) 454-8238
email: mcrc@pacbell.net
Donates computers and related equipment to schools, libraries, and nonprofits in the vicinity of Marin County. Six-month waiting list.

New Life Computer Foundation (NLCF)
24026 Gilmore Street
West Hills, CA 91307
tel. (818) 348-9264
fax (818) 348-9261
Los Angeles–based nonprofit that redistributes used computers to schools and nonprofits. No charge. Computers refurbished by volunteers. Volunteers provide technical training.

Appendix 2

Appeals Process

How to Appeal

As a parent, you have the right to appeal any action by the school's staff that you believe is unfair, inappropriate, unjustified, or illegal. Often, the easiest way to solve a problem is to talk privately and directly with the person with whom you disagree. If the two of you cannot come to an understanding, you'll need to appeal to their boss. If, for example, you're having a problem with your child's teacher or with any of the other staff in the school, you should appeal to the principal. On some issues, the principal is the final authority; however, most of his decisions can be appealed to the district superintendent, your local school board, and/or the county board of education.

Although appeals may be made orally or in writing, schools are required to respond only to written complaints. Many districts have developed a form for parents to use in filing complaints. While you are not required to use this form, the questions may help you organize your thoughts.

When filing a complaint, the important thing to do is to tell the complete story. Don't worry about grammar or spelling; just tell your story. A complaint letter should include your child's name, grade, and class; a clear description of the incident or situation (including the date and time); why you believe it is a problem for your child; and what action you want the person you're addressing to take. Describe any meetings or conversations you have held with the school and district to resolve the situation, the results of these meetings or conversations, and the names and positions of the people in attendance or with whom you've talked. Be sure to sign and date your complaint and keep a copy for your files. The principal has 30 days to respond to your written complaint.

The county office of education may also be helpful. However, with the exception of holding expulsion hearings, and providing special and vocational education, and schools for at-risk youth, county offices usually act in an advisory or supportive role to schools rather than as enforcement agencies. (County offices of education also monitor and approve school budgets, but that role is not relevant to the complaint process.)

California Department of Education's Complaints Management Services

When you are not satisfied with the answer you receive from your school or district, you need to appeal to the California Department of Education. (Although some state bureaucracies have appointed an ombudsperson to assist citizens in negotiating bureaucracies to resolve complaints, the Department of Education has not yet moved in that direction.) In California, Complaints Management Services (CMS), a department within the Department of Education, handles complaints from parents and students involving problems in most of the larger state-funded programs, including Title I, bilingual programs, school improvement programs, migrant education, special education, vocational education, and any civil rights violation. For example, if your child is academically below grade level and the school is not providing tutoring or other academic support, or if no one is listening to your concerns about your child's special education placement, you should consider filing a complaint with CMS. Your parent group also should call CMS when your school site council or district council is excluding parents from the decision-making process.

Some issues, of course, are not handled by CMS. Only the teacher may change your child's grade; suspension or expulsion decisions may not be appealed above the county level; and records decisions may not be appealed beyond the district level. If you have a question about the appropriateness of your appeal, call CMS and ask.

Here's how the CMS process works.

- If you are not satisfied with the response you received from your school district or if it has taken more than 60 days for them to respond, file a written complaint with CMS. You have 15 days after you receive the district's negative response, or 75 days from your initial appeal to the district, to file a complaint with CMS.
- After it receives your complaint, CMS will ask the local school district for a copy of: (a) your original complaint, (b) the district's de-

cision, (c) a summary description of the nature and extent of the district's investigation, (d) a report of any action taken to resolve the complaint, (e) a copy of the district's complaint procedures, and (f) other information CMS considers relevant.

+ CMS will then either help you and the district mediate the complaint, or conduct its own investigation of your complaint. If CMS finds the school district in violation of a regulation, it will provide technical assistance to the district to correct this violation.

+ Districts that reject the Department's decision may appeal to the State Superintendent of Public Instruction. Parents do not have the right to appeal.

Although CMS is pledged to protect your confidentiality and the facts related to the case, the Department is reluctant to accept anonymous complaints, and will do so only if the staff can be convinced that there has been harm done to the family filing the complaint.

In addition to its role in complaint resolution, CMS publishes a *Coordinated Compliance Review Training Guide* that is used to prepare school personnel, personnel from other school districts, university faculty, community members, and parents to assist in monitoring most major school programs. This document, over 350 pages long, defines what a school must do to carry out these programs and how to tell whether a school is in compliance with the law. You may call CMS to receive a copy of this training guide (there may be a charge). A review of this material will help you in the preparation of your complaint. The book is particularly helpful for parent groups who have been shut out of the decision-making process.

CMS's address and telephone number are:

> Complaints Management Services
> California Department of Education
> P.O. Box 944272
> Sacramento, CA 94244-2720
> (916) 657-2754

U.S. Department of Education's Office for Civil Rights (OCR)

If you feel that your child has been discriminated against because of her race, color, national origin, sex, disability, or age, you may want to consider filing a complaint with the Office for Civil Rights (OCR), a division of the U.S. Department of Education. OCR is responsible for enforcing the provisions of the federal laws prohibiting discrimination based on any of the above characteristics.

You may file a complaint by completing the Office's Discrimination Complaint Form (see below for contact information); you may also begin the complaint process by sending a signed, dated letter to the Office for Civil Rights containing the following information:

- the name, address, and home and work phone numbers of the person filing the complaint;
- your child's name, address, and phone numbers;
- the name and address of your child's school, and principal's name;
- the basis for your complaint—discrimination based on race, color, national origin, gender, disability, or age;
- a complete description of the incident(s): where and when—dates and times—and who was responsible; and
- the actions you have taken to resolve your complaint.

OCR is pledged to protect the identity of complainants; however, if OCR believes that this information is important to the investigation, you must be willing to have your name released to the school. OCR will not release your name without your written consent.

It can take from several months to several years to resolve an OCR complaint. If you'd like quicker action, the Office has instituted what's called the Early Complaint Resolution (ECR) process. ECR complaints are limited to charges that involve only one student (that is, group discrimination is not handled in this manner), and require that both the parent and district are willing to submit to mediation. After receiving your written complaint, the Office will judge whether the ECR process is appropriate for your charge and will ask you whether you are willing to pursue that option.

Address your complaints to:

> Stefan Rosenzweig, Regional Civil Rights Director
> U.S. Department of Education, Region IX
> Old Federal Building
> 50 United Nations Plaza, Room 239
> San Francisco, CA 94102
> (415) 437-7700

Index

Boldface page numbers indicate material is contained in boxes.

School Profiles Help You Choose Schools With The Facts In Your Hands

Whether you're searching for a new school or curious about your child's current school, this profile enables you to hold all the facts in your hands. In eight pages, you'll learn about teachers, students, and key resources in an easy-to-read format. Test score results, teacher-student ratios, teacher credentials, student language skills, and much, much more are compared to county and state averages. No educational jargon. No calculator needed. No risk of being out-of-date. Just $6 per school, plus tax and shipping.

School Rank Almanacs For Every California County

Here's the reference book designed to help you find the schools you want in your county. Get the advantage of an education insider. All public elementary, middle and high schools are ranked on over twenty criteria: teachers' experience, education, and credentials ... students' test scores, language skills, and ethnicities ... schools' enrollments, teacher-student ratios, computer-student ratios, average class sizes, and more. Over 140 pages of current school facts can be your guide through the maze of school choices in front of you. Data is always up-to-date because we print your book within one day of receipt of your order. Prices vary by county.

To order, call us at 800 247-8443, fax us at 415 337-1146, or e-mail us at sales@schoolwisepress.com

SCHOOL WISE PRESS
HELPING PARENTS GET SMART ABOUT CALIFORNIA SCHOOLS (K-12)